The French Novel of Quebec

Twayne's World Authors Series

French-Canadian Literature

David O'Connell, Editor
University of Illinois

TWAS 766

The French Novel of Quebec

By Maurice Cagnon

Montclair State College

Twayne Publishers • Boston

The French Novel of Quebec

Maurice Cagnon

Copyright © 1986 by G. K. Hall & Co.
All Rights Reserved
Published by Twayne Publishers
A Division of G. K. Hall & Co.
70 Lincoln Street
Boston, Massachusetts 02111

Copyediting supervised by Lewis DeSimone
Book production by Elizabeth Todesco
Book design by Barbara Anderson

Typeset in 11 pt. Garamond
by Modern Graphics, Inc., Weymouth, Massachusetts

Printed on permanent/durable acid-free paper
and bound in the United States of America.

Library of Congress Cataloging in Publication Data

Cagnon, Maurice.
  The French novel of Quebec.

  (Twayne's world authors series; TWAS 766. French-
Canadian literature)
  Bibliography: p. 145
  Includes index.
  1. French-Canadian fiction—History and criticism.
2. Québec (Province) in literature.   I. Title.
II. Series: Twayne's world authors series; TWAS 766.
III. Series: Twayne's world authors series. French-
Canadian literature.
PQ3912.C34   1986   843'.009'9714   85-27228
ISBN 0-8057-6617-0

For Armand Chartier,
thanks to whom . . .

For Stephen Smith,
without whom . . .

Contents

About the Author
Preface
Acknowledgments
Chronology

Chapter One
Introduction   1

Chapter Two
Pre–Nineteenth Century   5

Chapter Three
Nineteenth Century   8

Chapter Four
Twentieth Century   18

Chapter Five
Conclusion   142

Selected Bibliography   145
Index   154

About the Author

Maurice Cagnon is Professor of French and Quebec literatures at Montclair State College. He is the editor of *Ethique et esthétique dans la littérature française du XXè siècle* (Stanford University) and coauthor of *Idée Principale/Style Varié: Stylistique, Grammaire, Traduction* (Newbury House Publishers) and has written many studies on contemporary French and francophone prose and poetry. He is an officer of major national and international associations, has served as a member of editorial boards of learned journals, and as a Review Editor for *The French Review*. A former Woodrow Wilson Fellow and Fulbright Scholar, he is the recipient of American Philosophical Society and National Endowment for the Humanities Research Fellowships.

Preface

This volume, intended for the general student of literature and society, is the first English-language introduction to the Quebec novel, and the first book-length study in French or English devoted to a chronological overview of its development. The book dwells chiefly on the nineteenth and twentieth centuries, during which time the novel in Quebec took on its own forms and validity as a mode of writing.

While the work's focus is primarily literary in tracing the evolution of the genre through discussions of major writers, it also notes the links between novelistic endeavors and historical, sociological, cultural, and political realities. The volume analyzes dominant formal and thematic preoccupations in specific authors and periods and in Quebec prose literature as a whole. Further, it stresses such recurring themes as the "call of the North," religious patriotism, nature and geography, the rural-urban polarity, the opposition between reality and myth as well as that between the earth and the cosmos, and between quotidian existence and visionary utopias. For the post-1950s period, the poetic, political, and phenomenological currents are underscored as essential components of notable Quebec novels.

Throughout, the book presents authors in a chronological order based on the publication date of the first novel that I study by each writer. This order allows a clear overall sense of the novelistic ambience—the similar or different themes treated, the techniques assayed—within given time spans. The slight exception is for the "psychological novelists" of the 1940s so that they can be referred to as a group.

Given my aims and the space limitations of the Twayne format, the volume pretends to be neither definitive nor exhaustive. Novelists selected are those who, for various reasons, are generally considered to be the most important in the history of the Quebec novel. My personal critical judgment is also a factor: some writers are given less attention than might be expected, for I consider them less significant than is often thought; others are given more attention, for I deem them worthy of due critical study—their work has heretofore received insufficient notice or been the object of faulty perception.

Patently, not all novels of all authors could be included for discussion in an introductory study of this sort. The novels chosen are those that, by general consensus, are seen as the most representative, or the best, or, in some cases, those that I feel have been neglected and deserve greater critical examination.

The first mention of each novel gives the original French title, followed immediately in parentheses by an English translation; if the work has a published translation, the title is in italics; if no published translation exists, the title is my own and appears in roman type. Subsequent to this initial French/English cotitling, only the French title appears. In the Bibliography full publication information of what are, to the best of my knowledge, the most recent English translations immediately follows the French edition entry; for novels that have no published translations, my own title is provided in parentheses. Bibliographical listings are for those novels specifically studied in the text and do not necessarily represent a given author's complete output.

For smoother reading in English, the term *Quebec* is used adjectivally as the equivalent of the French *québécois*.

Maurice Cagnon

Montclair State College

Acknowledgments

I wish to thank editors and publishers for permission to incorporate revised versions of the following studies: "Parody and Caricature in Hubert Aquin's *L'Antiphonaire*," *Critique: Studies in Modern Fiction* 19 (1977):5–11; "Palimpsest in the Writings of Hubert Aquin," *Modern Language Studies* 8 (1978):80–89; "Devant l'écriture aquinienne: optiques et perspectives," in *Ethique et esthétique dans la littérature française du XXè siècle*, Saratoga, Calif., Anma Libri Press, 1978, 155–62; reviews of Gérard Bessette's *Le Semestre*, *French Review* 54 (1981):499–500; Yves Beauchemin's *Le Matou*, *French Review* 55 (1982):920–21; Gilbert La Rocque's *Les Masques*, *French Review* 56 (1982):172–73; "Louise Maheux-Forcier and the Poetics of Sensuality," *Quebec Studies* 1 (1983):286–97; "*Le Matou* d'Yves Beauchemin: une lecture idéologique," *L'Esprit Créateur* 23 (1983):95–104; "Louise Maheux-Forcier and the Poetics of Sensuality" in *Traditionalism, Nationalism, and Feminism: Women Writers of Quebec*, Westport, Conn., Greenwood Press, 1985, 95–107.

I extend my sincerest gratitude to: my editor and friend David O'Connell for his expert supervision and patient understanding; Anne Jones, Twayne Associate Editor, Elizabeth B. Todesco, Production Editor, and Lewis DeSimone, Manuscript Editor, for their superb work and gracious cooperation; Céline Dupré and Suzanne Dupré for their help in obtaining certain otherwise unavailable works; Régine Imsand for her prompt, impeccable manuscript typing; André Sénécal (University of Vermont), Emile Talbot (University of Illinois), André Gaulin (Laval University), Marie Couillard (University of Ottawa) for their general counsel and bibliographical help; Philip Stratford (University of Montreal), Eva Kushner (McGill University), Nancy Crane (University of Vermont library), Katherine Berg (Canada Council, Ottawa), Merle Fabian (Canadian Embassy library, Washington, D.C.), Francine Neilson (Bibliothèque Nationale du Québec) for their advice in tracking down English translations; John O'Connor (University of Toronto), who was especially helpful in this task and also in his thorough reading of the *Bibliography;* Charles

Mathews and Suzanne Lamy for their indispensable "logistical support." The Montclair State College Research Fund provided support time for the completion of this book.

Chronology

1534–1542 Jacques Cartier's expeditions.

1545 Cartier's travel narrative.

1608 Samuel de Champlain founds Quebec City.

1613 Champlain's travel narrative.

1632–1672 *Relations des Jésuites.*

1642 Montreal founded.

1681 Letters of Marie de l'Incarnation published.

1713 Treaty of Utrecht; England acquires Newfoundland, Acadia, and Hudson Bay.

1755 Deportation of Acadians begins.

1759 Montcalm's defeat on the Plains of Abraham; Quebec's capitulation.

1760 Capitulation of Montreal; New France in hands of British-American troops.

1763 Treaty of Paris; France surrenders New France to England.

1791 Constitutional Act separates Canada into two provinces (Lower Canada, present-day Quebec; Upper Canada, present-day Ontario).

1829 McGill University established.

1837–1838 Patriot's Rebellion in Lower Canada.

1840 Union Act reunites Upper and Lower Canada.

1844 Institut Canadien founded in Montreal.

1845 François-Xavier Garneau's *Histoire du Canada.*

1852 Université Laval established.

1853 Pierre-Joseph-Olivier Chauveau's *Charles Guérin.*

1860 Ecole Patriotique de Québec literary group created.

1863 Philippe Aubert de Gaspé's *Les Anciens Canadiens.*

1867 Confederation created by British North America Act.

1874   Antoine Gérin-Lajoie's *Jean Rivard le défricheur.*

1884   Laure Conan's *Angéline de Montbrun.*

1895   Ecole Littéraire de Montréal group founded.

1916   Louis Hémon's *Maria Chapdelaine.*

1918   Albert Laberge's *La Scouine.*

1920   Université de Montréal established.

1922   Abbé Lionel Groulx's *L'Appel de la race.*

1933   Claude-Henri Grignon's *Un Homme et son péché.*

1936   Union Nationale party created; electoral victory for Maurice Duplessis.

1937   Félix-Antoine Savard's *Menaud, maître draveur.*

1938   Ringuet's *Trente arpents.*

1941   Robert Charbonneau's *Ils posséderont la terre.*

1944   Duplessis's political reign until his death in 1959; R. Charbonneau's *Connaissance du personnage;* Roger Lemelin's *Au pied de la pente douce.*

1945   Pierre Baillargeon's *Les Médisances de Claude Perrin;* Germaine Guèvremont's *Le Survenant;* Gabrielle Roy's *Bonheur d'occasion.*

1948   Publication of artist Paul-Emile Borduas's *Refus global,* the Automatists' manifesto.

1953   Hexagone literary group created; André Langevin's *Poussière sur la ville.*

1954   Yves Thériault's *Aaron.*

1958   Anne Hébert's *Les Chambres de bois.*

1960   Liberal Party victory; "Quiet Revolution"; Rassemblement pour l'Indépendance Nationale formed; Gérard Bessette's *Le Libraire.*

1962   Jacques Godbout's *L'Aquarium.*

1963   Front de Libération du Québec (FLQ)'s terrorist attacks; *Parti Pris* journal created; Louise Maheux-Forcier's *Amadou,* first novel of trilogy.

1965   Hubert Aquin's *Prochain épisode;* Marie-Claire Blais's *Une Saison dans la vie d'Emmanuel;* Jacques Ferron's *La Nuit.*

1966   Réjean Ducharme's *L'Avalée des avalés;* Suzanne Paradis's *Femme fictive, femme réélle: le personnage féminin dans le roman féminin canadien-français.*

1967   Charles de Gaulle's "Vive le Québec Libre!" speech; R. Ducharme's *Le Nez qui voque;* J. Godbout's *Salut, Galarneau!*

1968   Parti Québécois (PQ) founded; creation of Bibliothèque nationale du Québec; H. Aquin's *Trou de mémoire;* Roch Carrier's *La Guerre, yes sir!,* first novel of trilogy; R. Ducharme's *L'Océantume.*

1969   First of controversial bills to establish French as primary and official language in province; H. Aquin's *L'Antiphonaire;* J. Ferron's *Le Ciel de Québec.*

1970   Robert Bourassa's Liberal Party comes to power; FLQ terrorism provokes repressive War Measures Act; A. Hébert's *Kamouraska.*

1971   S. Paradis's *Emmanuelle en noir.*

1972   Victor-Lévy Beaulieu's *Un Rêve québécois.*

1973   R. Ducharme's *L'Hiver de force.*

1974   V.-L. Beaulieu's *Don Quichotte de la démanche.*

1975   M.-C. Blais's *Une Liaison parisienne;* A. Hébert's *Les Enfants du sabbat.*

1976   Victory for René Lévesque's Parti Québécois; Louky Bersianik's *L'Euguélionne.*

1977   Charte de la Langue Française becomes law; G. Bessette's *Les Anthropoïdes;* S. Paradis's *Un Portrait de Jeanne Joron.*

1978   V.-L. Beaulieu's trilogy, *Monsieur Melville.*

1979   M.-C. Blais's *Le Sourd dans la ville;* S. Paradis's *Miss Charlie.*

1980   Defeat of Quebec's proposed sovereignty-association with Canada, a setback for Lévesque's party; Gilbert La Rocque's *Les Masques.*

1981   Yves Beauchemin's *Le Matou;* R. Carrier's *La Dame qui avait des chaînes aux chevilles;* J. Godbout's *Les Têtes à Papineau.*

1982   M.-C. Blais's *Visions d'Anna;* A. Hébert's *Les Fous de Bassan.*

1984   Resignation of Canada's Prime Minister Pierre-Elliott Trudeau.

1985   Resignation of René Lévesque as Quebec's Prime Minister and leader of the Parti Québécois.

Chapter One
Introduction

Through the end of the nineteenth century the slow and problematic development of the novel form in French Canada showed the considerable influence of France's classic and romantic traditions as it gradually evolved into a more and more autochthonous expression of French Canadian reality. The earliest prose writings in New France, however, were primarily travel narratives by explorers and discoverers, among whom the most important were Jacques Cartier and Samuel de Champlain. These works are invaluable as firsthand descriptive accounts of the geography and ethnology of the land in the sixteenth and seventeenth centuries. The *Relations des Jésuites* (Accounts of the Jesuits), written over a forty-year span (1632–1672), are hybrid mixtures of religious propaganda and historical chronicles, interspersed with narrative passages. Sister Marie de l'Incarnation's voluminous epistolary and religious writings in the seventeenth century are significant more for their documentary value as mystical tracts than as objects of the creative imagination.

Certain pivotal historical events in the course of the eighteenth and nineteenth centuries caused repercussions in French Canada's destiny that would be felt well into the present. Montcalm's defeat on the Plains of Abraham, the Treaty of Paris (which placed French Canada under British rule), and the failure of the 1837–1838 Rebellion provoked a dangerous, inward-looking, nostalgia-ridden attitude, an insidious process of submission-assimilation, which attempts at self-affirmation in the latter part of the nineteenth century would be unable to fully dissipate. Concurrent with British domination was the ascending, quasi-absolute power of the clergy, which regulated (i.e., formally, morally approved or condemned) virtually all artistic endeavors and considered the novel, in particular, as subversive and thus best reduced to hidebound conformity to Church teachings or else to total silence. With the Confederation Act of 1867 the land's inhabitants became "French Canadians"; the term *Québécois* (English "Quebecers") with its nationalist overtones,

1

new geographic awareness, and literary thematic expressions only
came into being during the "Quiet Revolution" of 1960.

Thanks to the Church's espousal of land development (land, language, and mores composing an inseparable unity of preservation),
the novel of the earth reached its apogee. It, too, would have a
lasting influence upon French Canadian letters, combining as it did
politics and religion to form an essentially messianic literature:
courage and solitude, acceptance and humility, tradition and faith
formed the unswerving vision of its mythos. In such representative
works as *Maria Chapdelaine (Maria Chapdelaine), La Terre paternelle*
(The fatherland), *Charles Guérin* (Charles Guérin) *Jean Rivard le
défricheur (Jean Rivard),* authors idealized their characters and offered
idyllic situations in which the sacred trinity is aspiration (to freedom), alienation (in an unforgiving land), and subservience (to Church
and God). During the first quarter of the twentieth century novelists
vacillated; some continued writing paeans to the land and peasant
way of life, others waxed noble and moralistic over value systems
of the past, still others indulged in poetic sublimations of agricultural hardships or, conversely, castigated the very tenets upon which
agriculturalism was premised. In the mid-twentieth century, primarily because of the social and economic facts of industrialization
and the urbanization that ensued, novelistic techniques, while vis-
ibly retaining residual continental French traces, became less nar-
rowly imitative. Realists like Roger Lemelin and Gabrielle Roy, in
both of whose first works World War II's consequences hold a
prominent place, sought more individualistic approaches for grap-
pling with pressing problems in Quebec as a geographic entity of
its own. Collective moral and cultural factors that had previously
articulated an agriculturist society now shifted to a rapidly growing
proletariat settled mainly in poverty-stricken areas of Montreal and,
to a lesser extent, Quebec City. Politics, or, more precisely, the
ethical implications of politics acquired heightened significance in
the urban novel as its characters had to wrestle both with an ingrained yearning for values and customs of the past and with over-
powering pressures of mysterious new socioeconomic systems and a
threatening, unfamiliar landscape.

The all-pervasive religious patriotism that infiltrated every art
form in the preceding century now gave way to a nationalistic, more
overtly political, areligious sensitivity. As the century wore on, this
nationalism, indeed, strongly colored and even served as an under-

pinning for major obsessive themes in the Quebec novel—themes such as defeat and oppression, death and salvation. After the so-called "Quiet Revolution" of 1960 and the subsequent advent of the "Parti Québécois" under René Lévesque's leadership, independentism became the sociopolitical byword. Writers in all the major literary genres responded to this clarion call; only in the mid-nineteen-eighties would a number of younger established novelists veer away from a vision of the future and rebirth and instead hark back to a notion of preservation based on heritage and patrimony.

In the 1950s and 1960s, novelists forged a new mythology that radically replaced the earlier backward-facing ideology; the liberalist political fervor of the period extolled a definitive decolonization of Quebec, and a rebuttal of the province's entrenched, rigidly fixed uniformity. Although (still today) combating redoubtable economic, political, and cultural counterforces, most novelists (and most of the enlightened intelligentsia) stress individual liberty within a context of an autonomous Quebec collectivity.

In this vein, Robert Charbonneau (who remains an underrated author), along with several other fictionists of the 1940s, had already reinvigorated the psychological novel form, in which conflictual human passions and unresolved beliefs in opposing ethical concepts supplanted a tendentious (Roman Catholic) humanism and its absolutist principles. Existential concerns also distinguished the evolution of the Quebec novel during the fifties and sixties, as authors tightened characterial links to background and milieu (proletarian milieu especially) that indelibly mark individual destinies. Novelists moved the sociopsychological novel toward psychoanalytical fiction and investigated heretofore untouchable taboos. Nonconformity was the password, often incarnated in rebellious adolescent figures who confront and reject adult representatives of an archaic moral and social order. France's "New Novelists" influenced Quebec's literary production in the 1960s and 1970s—novels deconstruct and fragment sanctified notions of time and space, character, plot, and narrative techniques. First-person narration displaced the third-person exclusive right to observe and recount; however, it is a decidedly flexible and ambivalent "I" and, in fact, not infrequently a thinly disguised collective "we."

Much of the novel's development from the 1970s to the present day has run in tandem with political events of the time. A yet more acute political awareness after the "Parti Québécois"'s ascendancy to power in 1976 was quickly muted by the party's defeat in the 1980 referendum concerning the provincial government's proposed sovereignty-association with the rest of Canada. The novel, which formerly displayed politically subversive propensities, tamed both its means and its ends. While structuralist and post-structuralist continental French influences remain manifest in the genre's formal architecture, a return to traditional techniques cannot escape attention, nor can a renewed emphasis on history and the historical novel of the type rampant in the nineteenth century. One of the major Quebec publishing houses has, symptomatically, defined the editorial policy of its "Quebec Novel" series as a return to regionalism and a creative inventory of Quebec's heritage. A cult once thought extinct seems again to be finding a privileged status in Quebec letters.

Chapter Two
Pre–Nineteenth Century

An agrarian, Catholic France founded New France in the early seventeenth century, colonizing the North American continent with peasants, noblemen, and bourgeois merchants. Along with these were numerous missionaries and nuns who established their communities and gave to the young nation the aura of doctrinal, religious vigor that would characterize its social and cultural institutions into the present century. In eighteenth-century French Canada landowners continued to reflect Frenchmen's abiding attachment to the land and uphold the strong tradition of faith; yet at the same time French Canadian peasants lived an insecure existence, faced as they were with the hardships of tilling the soil and with struggles against the Indians and the British.

Under British rule villages were established in the fertile Saint Lawrence valley, and French Canada definitively chose a rural economy, albeit one that did not always progress at sufficient pace. Stagnation, coupled with a severe rural overpopulation problem, later forced a vast emigration to the productive textile-mill towns in New England and the South. (When industrialization finally did come to French Canada, especially during World War II, it found the country sorely wanting in capital and in technological expertise.) The peasant and petit-bourgeois mental outlook not only penalized the French Canadians economically, but also significantly slowed down their cultural evolution, despite continuing links with the mother country. Education, under the dominance of the Jesuits since the end of the sixteenth century, slackened dangerously after the Conquest, and was not to be systematized by laws until the mid-nineteenth century. Indeed, even past World War II, French Canadian higher education was virtually limited to preparing for careers in law, medicine, and religion.

The creation and evolution of any "national" literature must be placed within the necessarily larger context of a country's evolving social institutions, its moral and ethical system, its economy and role in the world. In the case of French Canada, that literature was and is the expression of a French-language community's identity and survival on a predominantly anglophone continent.

Prior to the first half of the nineteenth century French Canadian prose was important as a corpus of historical documents (notably the writings of Jacques Cartier [1491–1557] and Samuel de Champlain [ca. 1570–1635]): explorers' chronicles, Jesuits' reports to French superiors of sundry apostolic activities in New France, the voluminous correspondence of the Ursuline nun Marie de l'Incarnation (1599–1672). A mystic, who was also acutely aware of her adopted land's development, she proved to be an exceptional witness to the history of French Canada. Such a Christian vision of the world, founded in a rigorous patriotic religiosity, was to dominate the French Canadian temperament until the twentieth century. These works possess undeniable documentary value but are slim in literary quality; moreover, their authors are French-born and French-trained. Almost a century was to pass before the birth of a truly native French Canadian literature. Under both French and British regimes specific conditions explain this slow gestation: sparseness of population, untoward climate, need to work the land and develop commerce, wars, lack of education, religious and linguistic dissidence. A dominant written form in the nineteenth century was journalistic prose, again affording reliable documentation of French Canada's national conscience but precious little literary interest.

With the Royal Proclamation of 1763 French law was relegated to silence; though French civil law was reinstated by the Quebec Act of 1791, the French language could not lay claim to official status (such recognition did not occur until 1849). For French Canada, then, the whole of the eighteenth century was a period of resistance against British and American submersion but, at the same time, one of gradual withdrawal and a growing inferiority complex. The entire social and political fabric of French Canada was dissolving: with the disappearance of the French legal system, the Church came under attack. Despite restrictions imposed by the British, that pillar of French Canadian education steadfastly remained the one real unifying force (and through the next century its greatest stultifying influence). Nonetheless, basic education was limited to the very few, and higher education was nonexistent; in 1852, with the founding of Laval University, French Canada was endowed with a complete educational system; in 1867 public education was put into the hands of provincial authorities. Given these circumstances, it may well be that journalism, history, and rhetoric were, in point of fact, better suited than poetry and the novel to state French Canada's social demands and assure its political and linguistic survival under British rule.

Chapter Three
Nineteenth Century

The novel in French Canada was slower still than poetry in creating works of lasting merit, because of continuing difficulties and obstacles of an economic, political, and educational order, but also because of a deeply ingrained and Church-influenced distrust of the novel form as pernicious to traditional French Canadian morality and ethics. François-Xavier Garneau's *Histoire du Canada* (History of Canada), published in 1845, at last provided the seminal work for an entire generation of writers who were to elaborate a genuine French Canadian literary tradition. These writers favored prose fiction of a decidedly nationalistic, patriotic nature, intermixing at will the historical, adventure, and thesis genres in the concoction of their writings. Examples of the primarily historical type are Philippe Aubert de Gaspé's *Les Anciens Canadiens (Canadians of Old)*, 1863; Napoléon Bourassa's *Jacques et Marie* (Jacques and Marie), 1865; Joseph Marmette's *François de Bienville* (François de Bienville), 1870; Honoré Beaugrand's *Jeanne la fileuse* (Jeanne the spinner), 1875. Of tales of extraordinary adventures, one can retain Philippe Aubert de Gaspé's *Le Chercheur de trésor ou l'influence d'un livre* (The treasure seeker or the influence of a book), 1837, sometimes cited as the first French Canadian novel, although perhaps hardly worth dwelling upon; Joseph Doutre's *Les Fiancés de 1812* (The fiancés of 1812), 1844; Pierre-Georges-Prévost Boucher de Boucherville's *Une de perdue, deux de trouvées* (One lost, two found), 1849; and Pamphile Le May's *Picounoc le maudit* (Picounoc the damned), 1878. Thesis or ideological novels of the period, with their heavy-handed pedagogico-didactic apparatus, are best represented by Pierre-Joseph-Olivier Chauveau's *Charles Guérin* and Patrice Lacombe's *La Terre paternelle* (both of which appeared in serial form in 1846), and Antoine Gérin-Lajoie's diptych *Jean Rivard le défricheur* and *Jean Rivard économiste* (in serial form in 1862 and 1864 respectively).

All of the same ilk, these prose works offer similar if not identical characteristics in content and form. As the psychological novel had not yet blossomed on French Canadian soil (Laure Conan's *Angéline de Montbrun* [*Angéline de Montbrun*] did not appear, in serial form, until 1881–1882), the characters undergo, for all practical purposes, no psychological evolution. Of a piece, they stand as rigid monuments of good or evil, as vehicles for some doctrinal or ideological stance that the omnipresent author never hesitates to underscore in asides to the reader or in blunt statements concerning key ideas, characters' conduct and attitudes, and sociopolitical situations which inform these texts. Characters' psychic fixity is carefully attuned to their stock physical traits: the hero who possesses every conceivable virtue is also endowed with every conceivable grace; the morally unfit are of necessity ungainly. To compensate for this characterial rigidity, authors of the period render the action of their novels as complicated as possible, with stupendous feats and miraculous coincidences abounding in all of them. In truth, the technique did not so much compensate for as further add to the hidebound aspect of the works; unfortunately, the legacy of such novelistic inflexibility was to persist well into the following century.

The agriculturist cult in nineteenth-century French Canada saw in the agrarian life-style and rural economy the source of personal happiness, a refuge against the evils of the world, the road to the fullest and finest realization of self. Such an ideological belief, all the stronger as it was willingly espoused by the majority of the province's leaders, went in tandem with the prevailing theology: the supposed simple, pure life of the husbandman carried out God's aims and will on earth. Counterbalancing this persistent myth was a significant refusal by many French Canadians of the notion that the land brought with it a decent life and sure hope for the future. By the late 1850s the exodus to prosperous American textile towns was sufficiently large for French Canadian rulers and clergy to mount a neocolonizing campaign that would populate rural areas heretofore untilled in the untamed North. It is against this general background that the novels of the century unfolded.

Pierre-Georges-Prévost Boucher de Boucherville (1815–1894? 1898?) and Napoléon Bourassa (1827–1916)

Boucher de Boucherville's *Une de perdue, deux de trouvées* appeared first in serial form between 1849–1851 and in 1864–1865, and was published in final version in 1874. An unbridled adventure story, the novel willfully complicates its plot in the extreme, multiplying narrative threads, arbitrarily juggling coincidences and reversals, episodes and intrigues. The work teems with authorial interventions as de Boucherville either plays out his role as character or steps in to reassure his readers on the correct interpretation of characters and situations. Divided into two volumes, *Une de perdue, deux de trouvées* takes place first in Louisiana and the Antilles and later in French Canada. In both volumes de Boucherville's descriptive talent is his saving grace; whenever he tries to deal with human emotions, or with history for that matter, he relies upon the tritest of techniques, and the novel consequently stumbles on its own mediocrity.

Napoléon Bourassa's *Jacques et Marie* was also first serialized, appearing in 1865–1866 prior to its publication in book form in 1866. Like so many formulaic novels of the period, *Jacques et Marie* focuses not upon a modest sphere of past or current history, but upon a larger panorama worthy of a "national" literature, specifically the history of the deportation of Acadians in 1755—the novel is subtitled *Souvenir d'un peuple dispersé* (Memory of an exiled people). The novelistic convention of the time prescribed an amorous intrigue, and Bourassa willingly grafted one onto the historical backdrop. Like Boucher de Boucherville, Bourassa excelled principally in his descriptive evocations, large tableaux of considerable visual force. Try as he might to imbue his work with psychological analyses, he fell victim to the melodramatic clichés that recur in virtually all the novels of the period. Characters do not evolve in time but rather permanently symbolize attitudes and reactions such as Patriotic Devotion, Perseverance, Fidelity to Land and Country. While Bourassa's stated desire was to incarnate the virtues and travail of a persecuted people, his written product borders on abstraction, not reality.

French Canada since the outset consistently chose to assert a "national" character and spirit that was often to enter into conflict with geography and history and that was staunchly based on French language, Catholic religion, and customs and traditions that had been gradually developing since the colonial era. The integrity and survival of a francophone people on an anglophone continent were at stake, and perhaps more instrumental than any other group in assuring this victory was the Catholic clergy, at least throughout the nineteenth century. It was the Church that structured the parochial and family life of French Canadians, guaranteed the diffusion of French by establishing a French-language educational system, and upheld traditions solidly entrenched in religious faith and practices. It was, however, these same fundamental spiritual priorities that, in large measure, stifled truly imaginative, innovative activity in the arts and in the novel in particular, condemned by the Church and often outrightly censored. French Canadian novelists well into the twentieth century remained unable or unwilling to free themselves of that imposed taboo so as to create a personalized literature that would transcend the level of orthodox or historico-patriotic prose and explode the literary quietude demanded by the Church.

It is not surprising then that the religious straitjacket, along with unfavorable historical circumstances, resulted in an understandably slow and, one could say, stealthy development of the novel form. While French Canadian writers were patently influenced—more so than many critics seem willing to concede—by French romanticism, realism, and naturalism, the influence was one of mediocre imitation rather than of creative affinity in reworking the vast store of autochthonous materials. Cowed by religious dictates (including those emanating from Catholic literary critics such as Abbé Henri-Raymond Casgrain, Adolphe-Basile Routhier, and Jules-Paul Tardivel) and political turmoil, French Canadian novelists veered away from a renewing aesthetics that would correspond to a new society and instead turned toward the past as guarantor of self and society.

In this mosaic three thematic fragments stand out which attracted novelists of the period: nature, family, and religion. For their purposes nature was twofold: a pastoral reality consisting of the farmland worked by the habitant along with the village, the congregation's center of rural life; and the untamed nature of the north country, the "pays d'en haut," a land of escape, danger, and discovery, roamed by adventurers (the coureurs de bois), trappers, and Indians. This natural polarity played an essential role in the French Canadian novelistic world into the twentieth century. Within the pastoral setting the nineteenth-century novel evoked or transcribed the customs and traditions, plights and struggles of the agrarian family unit, all the while justifying this sole meritorious mode of life. Nature and family were intricately linked to religion as the underlying principle of human thought and the great unifier of temporal and spiritual orders of life. Characteristically also, novels intertwined religion and patriotism as the fundamental and ultimate goal and expression of the French Canadian ethos. Two ancillary themes typically recur in variant forms in the historical, adventure, and thesis novels: geographical color and picturesqueness, and the sense of the marvelous. The first was inspired by the land itself—its awesome size, its remote wilderness, at once inviting and forbidding, its flora and fauna—and by a special flow of time—the cycle of seasons with their hardships and pleasures, their assigned work and allocated leisure. As for the marvelous, it was an atavistic sort of belief in the fantastic, with sources in history, legend, folklore, and the parareligious. The stupendous adventure story so popular in nineteenth-century French Canada was but another extension of this special sense, as was the obsession with sorcery and madness that reached well into the century to follow. These multiple themes crisscrossed in differing intensities and patterns in the works of Aubert de Gaspé, Gérin-Lajoie, Beaugrand, and Conan.

Philippe Aubert de Gaspé (1786–1871)

Les Anciens Canadiens (Canadians of Old), extracts of which appeared in 1862, was published complete in 1863; a revised and corrected version appeared a year later. Plot and action play a relatively unimportant role in *Les Anciens Canadiens*, as its author is primarily interested in setting forth his patriotic notions, sketching out canvasses of rural life, and evoking customs and traditions of his youth during the French regime. While the work is certainly of more historical than literary value, this is not to say that Philippe Aubert de Gaspé presents a verifiably accurate panorama of French Canadian history. In his predictable tableaux of rural life as the one peaceful, reassuring reality, the author usually idealizes rather than attests to the factual truth of place, people, and mores. The glorification process establishes a mythical aura about the daily life of his characters, among whom he weaves complex but purely exterior relationships, and who seem predestined to misfortunes, to living out ill-fated loves. The novel suffers from overuse of the narrative third-person past and from the author's omnipresence in an edificatory prose at the service of patriotic propaganda.

Antoine Gérin-Lajoie (1824–1882)

Jean Rivard le défricheur (Jean Rivard) was serialized in 1862, followed by *Jean Rivard économiste (Jean Rivard, Economist)* in 1864.

It was not until 1874 and 1876, respectively, that the works, in revised versions, were published as books. Antoine Gérin-Lajoie's work sees the greatness and future of French Canada in the will to colonize the land. The ideal of rural life in the fatherland alone can counterbalance the agricultural recession of the time, the overcrowded liberal professions, and the massive exodus toward American textile centers. However, as the title of his books indicates, Gérin-Lajoie's hero is not merely a *défricheur* (pioneer settler), he is also an *économiste*. Rivardville stands as a symbol of support for small businesses and local industries, for the creation of a self-subsistent community that makes every effort to build schools and staff them with competent teachers to educate its children and its adults. Gérin-Lajoie paints the urban, industrial life as an unequivocal danger and downfall, whereas the agrarian mode of life assures the safeguarding of French Canada's religion, language, customs, and traditions. The author sums up every commonplace formula that entraps most novelists during the century. As in other works, characters here do not evolve in any autonomous fashion; lengthy, static discourses on economic and agricultural matters often break up the narrative; dialogue is stilted and the tone moralizing. It is, in fact, difficult to conceive of this as a novel—the protagonist himself is relieved at not having been sullied by reading novels and considers contemporary literature absurd and false. Jean Rivard is not a believable character but rather a mythical personage illustrating the Colonist; Gérin-Lajoie's "novel" is rather an allegory of colonization, not a concrete rendering of the social climate of nineteenth-century French Canada.

Laure Conan (1845–1924)

Angéline de Montbrun (*Angéline de Montbrun*) first appeared serially in 1881–1882, then in book form two years later. Laure Conan (pseudonym of Félicité Angers), French Canada's first woman novelist, stands apart from all other writers of the century for having slipped out of its literary vise and authored a novel that is notable for inner-oriented psychological analysis rather than stereotyped patriotic, sociological, or apologetic preoccupations. As such, author and work are the single most important transitional link between nineteenth- and twentieth-century French Canadian prose (her writings span a fifty-year period, 1878 to 1925), Conan was, however, much influenced by Garneau's *L'Histoire du Canada* and the writings of the early Jesuits in French Canada, and, like her contemporaries, she considered a knowledge and appreciation of history and the nation's past as the touchstone of human understanding. This belief informs virtually all of her writings other than *Angéline de Montbrun*, none of which possesses anywhere near the psychological acuity of that work. The numerous hagiographies bear little relation to novelistic art; her three historical novels suffer from a cumbersome patriotic apparatus, rigid characterizations, and tedious grandiloquence. Underlying all these works is the author's fervent love of her native land, deep religious faith, and quiet resignation to inescapable suffering as the lot of the human creature.

Angéline de Montbrun reveals a transparently autobiographical transposition of the life of Félicité Angers, who lived most of her life in the isolated Charlevoix village of Saint-Etienne de la Malbaie where she was born. Pious, timid, and withdrawn, Conan, while not expressly saying so, viewed writing as a thinly disguised confessional mode of expression, though after 1882 she chose no longer to write novels in the psychological vein but turned instead to conventional religico-patriotic themes common to the literature of her century. *Angéline de Montbrun* does what novels until then had failed to do: it provides a penetrating study of one human personality, it seeks out and communicates in convincing analytic terms the inner truth of an individual destiny. For the first time a novelist personalizes French Canadian prose. So strong is Conan's identification with Angéline that the other characters serve as vehicles for analyzing more deeply the protagonist's anguish and inner struggle, her search for consolation and a certain peace in Christian resignation. This is a constant in Conan's heroines, all of whom seem doomed to suffering and all of whom find somber satisfaction and pleasure in that suffering. And just as Conan, after what appears to have been an ill-fated (i.e., never-consummated) love, devoted her entire life to history and hagiography, so also her heroines turn to patriotism and religion to rationalize or sublimate complexes with which they are unable to cope. That *Angéline de Montbrun* proved a sufficient exorcism for Conan or that the fear of public identification between the author's life and her character's situation became unmanageable (in the preface of the novel she violently rejected even allusions to her personal life) may well explain her decision to avoid the psychological novel form after this publication. Both author and character live an essentially inner life of uncommunicated hope and bitter disappointment; both revel in a willed solitude; both sublimate into a mystical passion their need for a perfect reciprocal human love.

Conan's novel is innovative in form as well as in content. The tripartite structure of the work begins with a section written in the epistolary genre: an exchange of letters among the four principal characters; the third and longest part is Angéline's diary, the protagonist's anguished analysis of self and situation. Between the two, Conan intercalates a brief third-person narrative which serves to bring the reader up to date on the two great misfortunes that have occurred (the death of Angéline's beloved father and her facial disfiguration due to a tumorous growth). Both the epistolary and diary modes relate facts, present characters, study attitudes and reactions without direct authorial intervention, thereby establishing a distance between author and character, reader and character, and granting the character fuller autonomy in her fictional time and space. Conan has so structured her novel that it can be viewed as Angéline's lengthy exploration of hazy subconscious regions in an attempt to convince herself of the impossibility of love after having intuited that very love as possibility. Rather than face a fragile fact, Angéline compiles a myth of certitudes that prohibit happiness: people, events, nature, Maurice himself to whom she attributes a failure to love, a repulsion for her because of her disfigurement, and, not unimportant, her love for her father which, after his death, she transforms into a veritable cult. Renunciation is resignation: Angéline, once locked into her solitude, ceases all efforts for or belief in a human-scaled happiness, fantasizing her suffering into an imagined perfect union with Maurice in the past, a continuing privileged moment with God and her father in the present. Angéline imposes upon herself the necessity not to yield to the desire for seeing Maurice and sharing their love; solitude is the supreme test for her during her long self-interrogation, by the end of which she has convinced herself of the ephemeral nature of happiness, of God's role in requiring separation and not union as the fact of life.

Conan's novel recounts her character's advance toward love and retreat from it once she perceives the precariousness of its daily existence. Thereafter, she remains in her moody contemplation of self and others, of love-as-tenderness, and the soul-states that that emotion causes to well up in her. Accounting for this attitude and for the only kind of love that Angéline is willing to admit are her sense of gnawing disquietude when she is faced with the reality of things and beings, a basic instinct to idealize everything in life, and a hypersensitivity that leads to alienation from the world about her. Having decreed that Maurice no longer loves her, having relegated love to the domain of religious reverie, Angéline lives in an isolation based rather more on disillusioned pessimism than on Christian faith. Conan is not merely the first woman novelist in French Canada, she is the first author to get away from historico-patriotic conventions in favor of psychological analysis, and the first to break the stereotyped female character in the novels of the period—not a mean feat for French Canadian letters in 1882.

The question of a French Canadian (of a "national") literature was discussed throughout the nineteenth century and especially after the publication, from 1845 to 1848, of Garneau's revelatory *Histoire du Canada*. With the renewed study of French Romantic writers, notably François René de Chateaubriand, Victor Hugo, and Charles Nodier, there evolved two influential schools or movements of the century. The first of these was the "Ecole Patriotique de Québec," composed of writers who wanted to give to French Canadian literature a new direction based on history, and the corpus of native legends, folk tales, and the oral tradition. Among those who frequented poet Octave Crémazie's bookstore in the city of Quebec were the novelists Chauveau, Bourassa, and Aubert de Gaspé, along with Abbé Henri-Raymond Casgrain, who fancied himself the group's spokesman and literature's chief critic. Two important journals emanated from these reunions: *Les Soirées canadiennes* (1861) and *Le Foyer canadien* (1863), both designed to restore pride in the past, a more acute awareness of history, and the creation of a specific literature indigenous to French Canada. If the group did not succeed in stimulating great literature, it did produce abundant writings through the remainder of the century.

Abbé Casgrain tried to adapt theological precepts to the notion of a national mystique founded on history and legend in order to ensure the salvation (in more than one acceptation of that term) of French Canadian writings. According to his dictates—and their effects were felt long after the movement's disruption—literature must be chaste and pure, religious in character, evangelistic in aim; it must reveal a people's devotion and faith, its noble aspirations and heroic traits. Love of nature and love of God often, indeed, replaced human affections in the literature of the century, a literature that retained a number of French Romantic characteristics (local color, picturesqueness, the legendary and visionary, evocation of the past) but dropped its confidential, confessional aspects (melancholy love, the cult of the "I," a sensitivity that exalted the imagination, and individualism).

In the 1860s the "Ecole patriotique de Québec" disbanded. Nevertheless, at the same time, a more socially oriented, militant Romanticism was flourishing in Montreal. National emancipation, political freedom, democracy, justice, and social progress were its passwords and the Institut Canadien its stronghold. Whereas the "Ecole patriotique de Québec" tended toward contemplation and mysticism, prose writers such as Gérin-Lajoie, Joseph Doutre, Arthur Buies, and Louis Fréchette extolled action and social utility, separation of church and state, and national sovereignty. After the breakup of the Montreal group, also in the 1860s, and prior to the "Ecole littéraire de Montréal," a strong current continued to build up in French Canada against French realism and naturalism in general, as against the novel form in particular. Poet Crémazie and critics Routhier and Tardivel violently rejected any literature that would separate the spiritual from the profane or exclude the religious from the political and social. A literary work could only be wholly moral in content and intent: such paraliterary criticism, based in its entirety on religion and patriotism, established morality as the sole and absolute criterion for the created work and refuted everything that was not apologetic or edificatory. (A curious paradox is that Laure Conan published *Angéline de Montbrun*—a "condemnable" psychological novel—at just about the time that this criticism reached its apogee.) It is to the credit of the "Ecole littéraire de Montréal," which bridged the nineteenth and twentieth centuries, that it espoused Romanticism and Symbolism in its desire to reinvigorate French Canadian literature. Created in 1895, it brought together poets and novelists, historians and critics in a collective movement that published *Les Soirées du château de Ramezay* in 1900 and, twenty-five years later, as the movement drew to a close, *Les Soirées de l'Ecole littéraire de Montréal*. Among its most important members one notes the poets Emile Nelligan and Jean-Aubert Loranger, and the novelists Honoré Beaugrand, Albert Laberge, and Claude-Henri Grignon. The latter two were to contribute significantly to the French Canadian novel in the first half of the twentieth century.

Chapter Four
Twentieth Century
1900–1950

Quebec society in the early part of the twentieth century perpetuated to a great extent the fixed ideology of the preceding epoch as set by the traditional elite cadre of professionals and clergy, though the effects of industrialization and urbanization gradually altered the economic and social substructure of the province. Concurrently, political leaders adopted a degree of authority heretofore reserved to the clergy. This new fact, along with an improved educational system, tended to create a more open public attitude and the beginnings of a greater freedom from clerical dictates and precepts. By and large, however, novelists continued to consider it a virtual duty to compose a literature praising doctrinal religious and patriotic themes. Nonetheless, the growing importance of Montreal as the province's metropolis, the numerous newspapers and learned journals publishing works in serialized format, and the various cultural associations' programs of lectures and literary evenings all lent themselves to increased intellectual and creative enterprises and interest among a larger public.

The still strong insistence upon preserving French language and culture in an anglophone milieu was made manifest in the person and writings of Abbé Lionel Groulx who, in reiterating the notions and aims of François-Xavier Garneau, became the spokesman and conscience of Quebec (his *L'Appel de la race* [The call of the race] dates from 1922). Again the master of the future had to be the past in the religico-patriotic sense; the danger here once more lay in a refusal to accept change and progress, in a tendency to search not for a people's tangible identity but for an outworn idealization of a collective self. The "Ecole littéraire de Montréal"'s avowed aim was to preserve the French language and to develop a national literature by creating a network of literary regionalism that would counterbalance the nefarious inroads of technological advances and resultant sociocultural decay. The forum for this campaign was *Le Terroir*, in which extracts of Albert Laberge's *La Scouine (Bitter Bread)* first appeared, and which was founded to illustrate through literary works the regionalist ethos.

Along with the "Ecole littéraire de Montréal," the "Société du parler français," as the name implies, sought to assure the survival and promulgation of the French language and of a literature closely identified with a nationalist ideology and the Catholic faith. Language and literature were seen essentially as modes of communication between church and society; preservation of the language was tantamount to preservation of the church and its influence in determining Quebec culture. The "Société du parler français" thus envisioned literature as the vehicle for glorifying nature, history, and liberty under a doctrinal, religious aegis. Abbé Casgrain and Abbé Camille Roy were the principal spokesmen for this crusade to nationalize Quebec letters, to create a national aesthetics based on the virtues, aspirations, and history of a "race." Familiar old spectres haunted and often halted the creative process as they locked the novel form into a matter of religious convictions, racial heroism and purity, historical and geographical grandiosity, to the detriment of any novelistic modes inspired by the French realistic-naturalistic tradition or the psychological novel. Although the ramifications of this concerted effort were wide and the effects long-standing, certain voices in the wilderness would be heard besides *Maria Chapdelaine*'s "Au pays du Québec, rien ne doit changer" (in Quebec, nothing must change), notably Albert Laberge's *La Scouine,* Ringuet's *Trente Arpents (Thirty Acres),* Gabrielle Roy's *Bonheur d'occasion (The Tin Flute),* Roger Lemelin's *Au pied de la pente douce (The Town Below).* Under the impact of Quebec's increasing industrialization the balance was to shift from the idealized rural novel of clerico-nationalistic aims to the urban novel, away from themes of geographic isolation toward those of a more individualized alienation.

Novelists such as Robert de Roquebrune and Léo-Paul Desrosiers carried on the tradition of the formulaed historical novel, while Louis Hémon, Damase Potvin, and Abbé Groulx persisted in producing idyllic novels of agrarian fidelity to the soil, inspired by a belief in an autochthonous literature composed of regional customs and conventions. Although Rodolphe Girard's *Marie Calumet* (Marie Calumet), 1904, took timid steps in the direction of an inner study of the individual self, not until Claude-Henri Grignon's *Un Homme et son péché (The Woman and the Miser),* 1933, do we find a semblance of the modern psychological novel, the first and sole prior example of which dates back fifty-two years to *Angéline de Montbrun*.

Louis Hémon (1880–1913)

Maria Chapdelaine (Maria Chapdelaine: A Tale of the Lake St. John Country) appeared first in serial form in 1914, and only in 1916, three years after the author's death, as a book. Louis Hémon, French by birth, writes with a precise realism that evokes the Lac Saint-Jean region—its milieu, customs, mores, the role of geography and the seasons—but also invokes the inner essence as well as the outer daily existence of the book's characters. Rather than merely describe his protagonist's behavior, or state her thoughts and emotions, Hémon manages to suggest Maria's psychic makeup as influenced by her spatiotemporal context: her ambivalent reaction to nature, her pious resignation to forces seemingly beyond her control, a certain kind of courage prompted by religico-patriotic voices urging her to remain faithful to the land and past traditions. The book's other characters are largely stylized figures symbolic of Maria's struggle. The father represents the pioneer spirit attracted to the adventure of opening up new forest land against all odds and difficulties; the mother yearns for the security and human communication of the village and parish life. François Paradis is the epitome of the coureur de bois whom Maria will continue to love even after his death and her projected marriage to Eutrope Gagnon, stoically faithful to the soil and understanding of Maria's plight. Lorenzo Surprenant, in the ideological dialogue between him and the mother, speaks for the wonders and amenities of the urban American scene of New England textile towns to which he emigrated.

What separates Hémon's work from earlier, less successful attempts at writing the rural novel is his awareness that he is not re-creating reality but creating the realistic illusion of that reality, an illusion based on two essential components, the evocation of an ill-fated love and the description of isolated rural life in the early part of the century, both of which are articulated about Maria as central figure and point of view. Maria's gaze upon things and beings as they affect her life gives meaning and power to psychological conflicts and to scenes of agrarian life around the remote Lac Saint-Jean. The characters' autonomy is, however, far from complete, for Hémon frequently interjects authorial interventions, mainly to brush tableaux of the collective milieu, its mental attitudes and customs, its idiomatic speech (here one senses Hémon the native-born French-man looking upon French Canada from the outside). Then Hémon becomes the omniscient author, filling in the reader on characterial and situational data unknown to his protagonist and giving his novel a certain resemblance to a sociological tract. The modulation of observation points cuts in on the immediacy and intimacy obtained when the book comes to us directly from Maria the character.

Hémon uses recurring concrete images to exteriorize Maria's inner psychological rhythms and to develop the book's principal themes. The epic, poetic "Song of the Earth" transcribes the notions of love and fidelity, patriotism and faith; the seasons and tasks that each entails symbolize man's nobility and survival; snow, cold, sounds (or lack of sounds) from the distant cascades, frosted windows, and the obsessional presence of the skirt of the forest (as the dividing edge between one life and another, between life and death), all attest to the stifling aloneness and separation that Hémon's protagonist comes to experience. These geographical and natural elements reappear throughout *Maria Chapdelaine* as tangible forms of inevitable fate, a bivalent symbol of solidarity and solitude, hope and despair, betrayal and redemption, a world open to the mysterious unknown and closed in on unchanging social and moral precepts. With *Maria Chapdelaine* Hémon brings the rural novel to a new apogee; the book as a whole and particularly the plaintive ballad with which Maria ends the work impart not a sense of apologia for a world that must at all costs be perpetuated but a note of nostalgia for a society that was soon to undergo an unavoidable metamorphosis.

Albert Laberge (1871–1960)

Excerpts of *La Scouine (Bitter Bread)*, in the guise of variously titled short stories, appeared between 1903 and 1916. As early as 1909 Albert Laberge incurred the condemnation of the Archbishop of Montreal for what was deemed to be material morally unfit to be printed. Hence the book did not appear in its complete version until 1918 in a private limited edition in Montreal.

Laberge's contemporary Damase Potvin (1882–1964) did not incur the Church's wrath, glorifying as he did the religious and na-tionalistic virtues of colonization and idealizing ancestral customs and the agrarian mode of life. As opposed to Laberge's vision in *La*

Scouine, Potvin, in *L'Appel de la terre* (The call of the earth) which also appeared in 1918 and which he subtitled *roman de moeurs canadiennes* (novel of Canadian mores), stresses the themes of local color, traditions of French Canada, fidelity to the soil, and happiness and love as found only in that fidelity. In this, his most famous work, as in the others that he authored, Potvin prolongs the stasis favored throughout the nineteenth century. The novelistic content is entirely keyed to the religico-patriotic formula, the intention is strictly apologetic, there is no invention to speak of—a near-total absence of attempts at analyzing events and characters, a lack of any sense of the novel's development in time, accompanied by a persistent judgmental authorial attitude.

Amid such continuators of a form and tradition already entrenched and Church-approved in the nineteenth century, Laberge's *La Scouine* heralds a significant step forward in the evolution of the Quebec novel. A disciple of the realist-naturalist school, Laberge infuses his novel (and short stories) with a sense of objectivity in observation and description hitherto deliberately avoided in prose works, that does not appear again until Claude-Henri Grignon's *Un Homme et son péché* in 1933 and Ringuet's *Trente Arpents* in 1938. It is, in this respect, interesting to note that *La Scouine,* begun in 1899 and finished in 1917, straddles two centuries just as it partakes, in its structure, of the novel and short-story form. Laberge architects the work in thirty-four sequences, the shortest composed of a single paragraph, the longest running to several pages. What this narrative technique may lose in gradual organic linkage, it gains in instant dramatic threads by cunningly choosing only the most highly charged gestures, attitudes, and words of his characters, all carefully related to their tawdry rural milieu, so as to reveal base, ambitious beings who ultimately become the victims of their own worst instincts. Where previous rural novels erected idyllic characters and surroundings in an aura of sociomoral ascension, Laberge sees humans as caught up in an implacable scheme of misery and mediocrity leading to moral and social decay. Tilling the soil is a thankless, unproductive task in an existence that is no more than a long period of servility, the term of which is shame, downfall, or death. The very pettiness of Laberge's characters and their anemic inability to react to their fate betray one of the darkest pessimisms in Quebec letters.

One ideological vision replaces another: whereas numberless other rural novels put characters and their milieu on a pedestal, *La Scouine* puts them on trial—and finds them irrevocably guilty. Torn from their agricultural habitat and forced to live in the nearby village, old Maço and her two children, Paulima and Charlot, are thereby stripped of whatever individuality they might have had, for their whole existence is chiseled out of the land and the toil it necessitates. The book's formal division into multiple tableaux enhances the objectivity and verifiableness that Laberge, like any self-respecting realist, wanted to impart to his novel. This ensemble of tableaux, carefully constructed according to notations and accumulations of precise details on characters and decor, inexorably builds the author's case against certain mores and a certain mode of life. Laberge does not analyze but observes what he considers the determinism that dictates the entire agrarian life and enslaves its practitioners. In form and in content, Laberge's book makes an ineradicable mark on the evolution of the Quebec novel, although both book and author were either passed over in cold silence or harshly admonished at the time.

The World War and the economic crisis in the 1930s exacerbated problems and accelerated changes that had been at work for some time in Quebec society, notably the mass exodus from farm and forest to city, and the severe unemployment and housing shortage in urban areas, resulting in poverty and misery for the growing working class. The Catholic Church, not wishing to lose its ideological hold upon society, undertook important social reforms. Organizing workers into numerous unions, its aims were to keep Quebec independent and French, its principles were respect for civil and religious authority. Concurrently with this worker movement, there evolved a policy of neocolonization of then-remote northern areas (Abitibi, Rimouski, e.g.) to encourage agriculture. The mythology of the *pays d'en haut* (the great north) dating from the previous century took on new life and meaning, though it may not have realized significant long-range results. The church, not surprisingly, strongly backed this return to the soil, to a supposedly saner, simpler way of life. Governmental and clerical approaches and positions overlapped as church and state further elaborated François-Xavier Garneau's notion of doctrinal nationalism and its inherent values: language, religion, family, agriculture. Abbé Lionel Groulx, one of the principal spokesmen of the time, set forth the historical thesis once again: history dictates the need for linguistic and political independence as a "nation" to protect against American encroach-

ment or immersion in an anglophone confederation. The period is
most importantly marked by an intellectual reevaluation of Quebec's
nationality in a larger political structure, of its creativity in literature
and the arts; in both, a strong sense of individuality emerges that
heralds the "Quiet Revolution" of the 1960s and the greater liberation which that "Quiet Revolution" brings about.

From a literary standpoint the 1930s and 1940s are a pivotal
moment in the evolution of Quebec prose, bringing to its natural
death the lengthy tradition of novels of adventure, history, and the
earth while simultaneously taking tentative innovative steps in novelistic techniques. Félix-Antoine Savard's *Menaud, maître draveur
(Master of the River)* and Ringuet's *Trente Arpents* undertake a final
inquiry into the themes of conquest, possession, and working of the
land. The notion of survival or renascence through fidelity to the
earth, which reached its culmination in Hémon's *Maria Chapdelaine*
and which had already been attacked in Laberge's *La Scouine,* was
further dismantled by Ringuet's realist-naturalist observation. Also
of consequence to the development of the novel was the appearance
of Grignon's *Un Homme et son péché,* published in 1933, five years
before *Trente Arpents.* Germaine Guèvremont's *Le Survenant (The
Outlander)* and *Marie-Didace (Marie-Didace)* shifted the focus of attention from the *défricheur de bois* (pioneer forest settler) to the dweller,
the habitant, of agrarian villages, from naturalist description to
psychological evocation.

Robert de Roquebrune and Léo-Paul Desrosiers valiantly attempted to prolong the life of the adventure novel, Roquebrune
drawing upon past historic events, not to exalt the earth, but to
sound the call to the mother country. Desrosiers chose the historico-
rustic mode as in *Nord-Sud* (North-South), 1931, or epic nobility
as in *Les Engagés du grand portage (The Making of Nicolas Montour),*
1938. Neither author succeeded, except in demonstrating that a
long-cherished novelistic tradition had indeed been drained empty.

Claude-Henri Grignon (1894–1976)

Un Homme et son péché (The Woman and the Miser) appeared in 1933.
Like Laberge before him, Claude-Henri Grignon, whose importance
cannot be overestimated, broke in significant ways with the realist-
naturalist tradition of the Quebec novel. Both abandoned the preconceived mold of the patriotic, moralistic eulogy of land and

habitant; neither subscribed to the idealizing vision and mission that marred so many "earthbound" novels of the previous century. In this respect, both Grignon and Laberge stand as pioneers and precursors of a realism more closely attuned to reality, a novelistic approach in which the plausible overlaps the verifiable; and that, even if Grignon's *Un Homme et son péché,* in particular, reveals drawbacks of oversimplification.

Grignon has no a priori axe to grind, no thesis to prove; rather, he makes a searching, clinical examination of one specific "case," that of Séraphin Poudrier who is driven to obsession by the "sin" of avarice. He bases his study on firsthand information of a reality that he professes to have experienced personally in the *pays d'en haut.* Grignon's technique is thus to avoid the impositional stance common to nineteenth-century novels: the global plot of *Un Homme et son péché* flows from within the book rather than being imposed from the outside; other characters' attitudes and reactions, events and situations, stem from the protagonist's personality and temperament. Grignon is not entirely successful, but his effort is commendable.

The author reconstructs his central character from what he avers to be three similarly afflicted persons known to him. He localizes Séraphin in a not-unfamiliar village in the Laurentians. Once having presented his wholly undifferentiated protagonist, Grignon inventories a multitude of evidential details to reflect Séraphin's single-minded obsession. By this method of careful selection of the intensity and hierarchical weight of objects surrounding a character, Grignon seeks to authenticate the meaning and ramifications of that character's psyche and actions. Rather than pay for medical treatment in time to save his seriously ill wife, Séraphin occasions Donalda's death, which closes one part of the novel and allows the entrance of cousin Alexis, his wife Arthémise, and their daughter Bertine. Their generous and loving presence aerates the monolithic dimension imparted to the text by Séraphin's monomania; it also diminishes some of the book's dark cynicism in a way that Laberge's characters did not do in *La Scouine.* Yet Laberge's worldview, as unabatedly pessimistic as it may be, is more convincing than Grignon's, for the latter's protagonist is too extremely stylized and stereotyped to be accepted as an avaricious person; he is instead the abstract notion of Avarice. This short-circuiting of the character's believability has a corollary shortcoming in the text's ultimate fictional event. Séraphin's house catches fire; he rushes in to save his gold and dies with it in hand. Grignon's regrettable recourse to so naive and embarrassing an accidental unhappy ending further adulterates the realism and reality of *Un Homme et son péché*—a realism and reality that were, to begin with, Grignon's stated aim in writing his novel.

Félix-Antoine Savard (1896–1982)

Félix-Antoine Savard's novels are noteworthy principally for their poetic descriptions of nature, their contemplative, lyrical quality. The author continues in the tradition of the novel of the earth with his tried and tired apologetic, religico-patriotic works. Plots are slim, ideas simplistic, characterizations shallow. Everything appears to be drawn into or overwhelmed by the natural context and religious beliefs, both of which lend to Savard's novels an epic, cosmic dimension. So preoccupied is he with language and style that he reworked *Menaud, maître draveur (Master of the River)*, 1937, over a period of twenty-seven years, a second version appearing in 1944 and the final, definitive version in 1964. *L'Abatis* (The felling), 1943, is rather more an extended lyrical meditation, a kind of innocent paean to man's sense of awe and discovery than it is a novel in any ordinary sense of the term. Its many short nature pictures and religious chants attest to Savard's mystico-poetic bent.

Menaud, maître draveur tells the tale of Menaud, the old hunter, trapper, and *draveur* (logger), a patriotic zealot who bitterly opposes the takeover by foreign interests of what he considers to be exclusively francophone Canadian soil and business enterprises. His daughter Marie is, not unlike Maria Chapdelaine, courted by a betrayer (he has sold his soul to the British) and a believer (who remains faithful to his etiology). Menaud's resistance campaign fails and the book closes on an ominous, yet feeble note of caution for Quebec—feeble because Menaud wishes to eternalize a world of past dream and myth instead of advancing a vision of the future. *Menaud, maître draveur* elaborates a long nationalist metaphor of the francophone Canadian "race," a metaphor that weakened the whole lineage of nineteenth-century novels of the earth with their similar personifications of soil and nature in the image of God. The end-note of despondency paradoxically demolishes the very thesis that Savard wanted to promulgate; if one accepts this reading, then the novel is less a warning against all social changes and more an appeal to recognize the inevitability and need for such changes. Savard draws up an implicit accusation of agricultural stagnation, not a glorification of agrarianism; fidelity to ancestral traditions brings with it merely the illusion of freedom and autonomy, a continuing enslavement within an evolving society. The theme is strong; it would have been stronger still if the poetic preoccupation had been less dominant. Savard's sensorial imagery establishes itself in an adversarial relationship with thematic content and ultimately attenuates the work's impact.

La Minuit (1948), that is, midnight of Christmas eve with its attendant religious symbolism of renascence and redemption, similarly begs the question by sabotaging its initial intention. A pall of fatalism is cast over the work as Savard seems not to be able to surmount a fundamental pessimism or allow his characters to free themselves from crippling resignation and dejection. Their reaction to the social and religious dialectics of *La Minuit* is one of humble submission to the social order, of paralyzing belief in a better life beyond. Corneau and Geneviève—the first an urban, diabolical figure, the second a pious habitante—serve to convey the author's convictions. Refusing to expect and wait for religious clemency and a higher order of justice, Corneau militates in favor of social reforms to counteract the abject misery that is rife in industrialized centers as well as the debilitating poverty and stasis of rural areas. He preaches human solidarity as opposed to religious quietude, the immediate overthrow of sacrosanct notions and laws which have proven to be defective. He preaches—but the flock does not heed; Corneau's proposed value system is thus as ineffectual as the one he seeks in vain to combat, and the novel ends in an impasse of understanding and communication. "Christmas eve" brings not redemption but stagnation and death.

Ringuet (1895–1960)

Well within the realistic tradition, Ringuet (pseudonym of Philippe Panneton) effects no revolutionary changes in the novel form, although he does bring to it significant refinements that are not without influence upon writers who will follow. *Trente Arpents (Thirty Acres)*, 1938, is closer to Laberge's *La Scouine* than it is to Grignon's *Un Homme et son péché* in that it presents less a case history of one man's obsession than a larger overview of rural society. Ringuet attempts to impart truthfulness and objectivity to the reality that forms the geographical and social context of his novel. He depicts agrarian life devoid of those preconceived ideological and social notions that, in the past, had imposed themselves on novels at their outset. Themes grow from inside the novel, gradually elaborating a kind of allegory of the habitant's fate during a trying period of mass emigration to American textile towns and increasing urban industrialization in Canada itself. In "Spring" and "Summer," the first two parts of the book, hopefulness and optimism preside over protagonist Euchariste Moisan's fate; "Fall" and "Winter," on the other hand, trace Moisan's downfall and dispossession.

Ringuet molds his characters in terms of the social and historical cadres in which they are immersed. Unlike their nineteenth-century novelistic counterparts, characters develop here progressively and organically in subtly evolving time and space. Although they are more personalized than in *La Scouine* and especially *Un Homme et son péché*, they nonetheless remain locked into a deterministic destiny and, as in Grignon's novel, are able to react to but not against their fate. Ringuet injects this same sense of evolution into discourse and situation: moving away from the omniscient author role, he modulates point of view by varying his characters' analysis of self and others in close accordance with specific situational contexts. Similarly, he abandons the purely narrative or discursive mode in favor of more flexible individualization of description and dialogue based on a given textual specificity. This is not to say that the novel achieves characterial autonomy or the situational open-endedness that will occur in more recent Quebec prose, for Ringuet's intent was to focus upon precise notation and accumulation of objects, gestures, and data in order to paint a vast collective portrait of agrarian society. It does mean that the author refuses the judgmental pose common to his predecessors; Ringuet resists a detailed psychological analysis of his characters based on religious principles, just as he rejects moral approval or condemnation of individual behavior and social attitudes.

Ringuet, and Germaine Guèvremont after him, put on record the end of an era in Quebec, with, however, this essential difference: Guèvremont's *Le Survenant* and *Marie-Didace* encompass only the rural geography of the Chenal du Moine area of Sorel as the author writes of the demise of the Beauchemin dynasty, whereas Ringuet's *Trente Arpents* follows Moisan in his journey from his devastated farmland to the desolation and poverty of his American urban exile. Seen from this perspective, Ringuet is a transitional figure leading away from the rural novel, solidly entrenched in a past reality, to the urban novel squarely facing an equally, but differently ruthless world soon to replace the old. Unlike earlier novelists of the rural genre, Ringuet depicts neither an idyllic agrarian life nor a wholly adverse urban existence. Nonetheless, in the dialectics of possession and dispossession which the novel unravels, Ringuet clearly and definitively stresses that his protagonist's voluntaristic attitude toward beings and things will not prevail. Moisan loses his land to his greedy son, experiences the lonely and tawdry life of a night watchman in a strange country, and supports his son Ephrem who has become an unemployed textile worker. Furthermore, Moisan will not ever return to his beloved homeland except in daydreams of what once was and no longer can or will be. Moisan is the possessed, the land and the city the possessors, as their spatiotemporal modes determine the psychological, social, and moral destiny of the uprooted, moving their victims from prosperity to misery, from youth to old age, from an idealized existence in the past to an uncertain life in the future. Ringuet, in addition, disengages the timeworn lever that links possession of land with a deep-seated love of nature, with a noble ideal of land-as-country, and retains only the equations: possession = instinct of survival, dispossession = certitude of death.

Roger Lemelin (1919–   )

Au pied de la pente douce (The Town Below), 1944, is the first Quebec novel to have a wholly urban geography as its locale—the working-class neighborhood in Quebec City's "Basse-Ville." Roger Lemelin's tone is so broadly humorous that his satire of society borders on caricature. In his sociological novels he depicts the strengths and failings of the working class and the lower middle class with a causticity that avoids being prescriptive. Not particularly adept at coordinated plot development, and indulging in cold leftovers of the intricate intrigues of the old adventure-yarn genre, Lemelin, like his nineteenth-century ancestors, is most successful in descriptions of large-scale tableaux, crowd activities engaging many or all of the inhabitants of Saint Sauveur, arresting collective portraits of a certain socioeconomic level. On the other hand, individual characterizations fall short of the mark, lacking in inner cohesion and cogency. What Lemelin's talent lacks in matters analytical it possesses in the visual; just as he brushes striking panoramas, so also he brings characters to life by his judicious perception of cardinal physical traits, tics, and gestures expressive of moral, mental, or emotional qualities.

In *Au pied de la pente douce* Lemelin divides the classes in question into two groups, the *mulots* (workers) and the *soyeux* (petits bourgeois), thereupon portraying the outer social interplay between the two and, more feebly, grafting onto the strong satirical background the story of Denis Boucher's love for Lise Lévesque (unlike him, one of the *soyeux*), and his aspirations to become a writer and rise above his social condition. Indeed, the novel in its time and space is articulated about this adolescent character; its fictional universe is structured by his efforts to live in reality what he thrives on in dream. The graft remains weak, for while it is through Boucher's gaze that we observe the innumerable fragments of Lemelin's novelistic world in an evolving present that is new to Quebec fiction, that gaze never peers within characters' psyches to search for root causes and reasons for behavior and motivations. Lemelin's outer-directed vision is a sweep of social strata discerned with noteworthy humor and healthy satire.

Like *Au pied de la pente douce, Les Plouffe (The Plouffe Family)*, 1948, is laden with excessively complicated story lines, and like the earlier novel it is most effectual in its depiction of vast frescolike scenes. Although Lemelin personalizes his characters, at times giving them somewhat more logical and psychological individuality than their counterparts in *Au pied de la pente douce,* they nevertheless tend to be static representations of specific social or political views. Theophile Plouffe is a printer at *L'Action chrétienne,* the quasi-official Church newspaper, and Denis Boucher is first a reporter for the same newspaper before writing for *Le Nationaliste.* Lemelin makes his characters mouthpieces for nationalism, francophone Canadianism, anti-Americanism, unionism, war, and draft registration. Pastor Follèche is treated even less sympathetically than he was in the first novel, while Boucher still fires his hopes upon writing the great Quebec novel, though he is here a relatively ancillary character outside the Plouffe family nucleus. But the reader experiences difficulty in accepting any of the characters and many of the situations seriously, since the book, by and large, takes on the tone of caricature, often in fact veering to burlesque. Lemelin succeeds in writing not so much a quotidian epic of the working class as a larger-than-life chronicle in the mock-heroic style. Whether intended or not, Lemelin's stress on the disproportionately ridiculous establishes a distance between book and reader, and a rapprochement with the author-satirist who offers a spectacle for facile delectation rather than a moving drama of a chosen social level during the onerous historical period from 1938 to 1945.

Germaine Guèvremont (1896–1968)

Germaine Guèvremont's novelistic output is not any the less important for being relatively slim; in addition to two novels, a collection of short stories appeared four years prior to *Le Survenant (The Outlander)*, 1945. The author's novel-diptych avoids the stereotyped pitfalls of the land-inspired novel tradition; it is in neither the religiously patriotic mold of *Maria Chapdelaine* nor the idealized thesis mode of, say, Gérin-Lajoie's *Jean Rivard*. Guèvremont, moreover, does not adopt the bleak realist-naturalist optics favored by Laberge and Ringuet; hers is, instead, a quiet, nostalgic statement, poetic and personal, about a sociological phenomenon in its twilight. Throughout her two novels the aging family head Didace Beauchemin is forced to ponder the extinction of the peasant clan that bears his name and, symbolically, the erosion of agrarianism as the dominant social component. But neither *Le Survenant* nor *Marie-Didace (Marie-Didace)*, 1947, is mere reportage of the documentary sort; and Guèvremont takes care not to cast either "Venant" in *Le Survenant* or "l'Acayenne" (the Acadian woman) in *Marie-Didace* as heroic figures. She uses but does not abuse local color and picturesqueness of the Sorel area in pointillistic fashion to highlight individual character traits or specific plot developments. Guèvremont's habit of composing her texts at the writer's inspiration, in juxtapositional order, enhances this pointillistic effect on the novels' spatiotemporal relationships. Blocks of time move forward, shift backward, then resume their propulsive motion; characters are spotlighted in precise gestures or verbal reactions or physical particularities that reveal their mental and emotional textures more acutely than psychological analysis, in which Guèvremont prefers not to indulge. By accumulating anecdotal scenes and dialogues the author evokes the claustrophobic world of the Chenal du Moine and the catastrophic awareness of consequences that the Survenant's quixotic sojourn prompts in such characters as Didace, Alphonsine, Amable, and Angélina. Guèvremont's study of the waning agricultural village life in Quebec, of the havoc wrought upon its xenophobic habitants by two strong-willed outsiders is as devoid of value judgments as it is of those predicatory stances inherent to the rural novel tradition in the preceding century.

Le Survenant is patently not a regionalist novel. While an important component of the work is its study of Sorelian society, it is far more essentially the study of individual independence and personal alienation. Guèvremont's writing subtly dovetails the Survenant's need for limitless but responsible freedom and the habitants' atavistic isolation. That is, the drama is such that one is played against the other, for the habitants feel fully comfortable in their seclusion, whereas the Survenant always senses the uneasiness of his aloneness among others. The psychological dialectics are, however, complicated by the fact that, in unstated but transparent ways, the Survenant is attracted to Didace, Angélina, and Alphonsine just as the latter are drawn to him out of admiration, gratitude, and love, respectively. Because the Survenant seems at once to entertain a close bond to the earth and manual work and yet be a free spirit, because he appears to be an aimless outlander but possesses a clearcut vision, he baffles those of sedentary bent and stirs up their hostility. Guèvremont in her definitive version of the novel (1968) chose to underscore the elusive nature of her central character by removing from the work a number of clues that robbed him of the mystery of his identity. She thereby preserved intact the legendary, mythical dimension emanating from the Survenant, the sense of hypnotic fascination, and she heightened the poetic aura of her work.

Le Survenant is not merely a novel of independence but also of difference—the need to be different, the enmity that difference provokes in those who fear it. To the stranger are alternatively applied various epithets: "wild man," "silent one," "bird of ill omen," "Great God of the road." Like Vincent Douaire in Nord-Sud, the Survenant is a wayfarer figure, an errant adventurer in search of renewal, refusing the stifling existence based on social constraints and financial security. His is the poet's cry of revolt against thralldom in a larger philosophic acceptation, against drudgery in a more pedestrian sense. Although he works with Didace, opens his soul to Alphonsine, his heart to Angélina, and joins in village gatherings, a basic dephasing always keeps him at a remove from the reality that surrounds him and that he refutes as a daily sameness, a persistent smallness. The difference resides in his unquenched need for departure and distance, space, and the unknown to be discovered. Inordinate pride and sense of superiority are manifestly keys to his authentic realization of self at the same time as they are factors in alienating others and preventing what he feels to be a contamination of himself by others. If no solidarity whatever exists between the Survenant and the village folk, it is because the protagonist does not perceive any possible meaningful solidarity; if no true communication ever evolves between him and the Beauchemin family with whom he lives, it is because he refuses as inadequate and inadmissible any communication that might be offered. Unwilling to bend under the yoke of social demands or emotional attachments, he leaves the Chenal du Moine as secretive and ambiguous as upon his unexpected arrival. Having eliminated from the novel those elements that too closely defined her protagonist, Guèvremont brings to the forefront a figure of haughty loneness who is destined to roam the world and establish connections with that world solely according to the dictates of his own free will.

In contrast to the rather grand scale of Ringuet's *Trente Arpents,* *Le Survenant*'s scope is a modest, when not intimate inquiry into the inner psychic domains of its principal characters. Guèvremont closes the circle even more tightly in *Marie-Didace.* The narrative function given the Survenant is here assumed by yet another stranger from an outside world held in suspicion by the Beauchemin clan and the villagers of the Chenal du Moine. Blanche Varieur, "l'Acayenne," while physically absent from *Le Survenant,* was, in truth, introduced to old Didace by the outlander himself, and the threat she poses to Alphonsine's already precarious self-esteem is stressed by her link with Guèvremont's antihero. Indeed, this rapport ties in the themes and situations of the two novels, both protagonists being not only outlanders in a hostile environment but catalytic figures working cataclysmic transformations in the social and psychological lives of those with whom they come into contact. Angélina's love for the Survenant amounts to a paralyzing affliction; Didace's acceptance of him as a surrogate son renews his hope for perpetuating the Beauchemins' place in the sun, if not the race itself—that hope only to be dashed by the Survenant's sudden, unexplained departure.

"L'Acayenne"'s entrance into the house, hitherto Alphonsine's stronghold, radically corrodes the latter's behavior, as it becomes motivated by jealousy and envy. In collusion with her husband, Amable, Alphonsine seeks only to undermine Blanche's influence for fear of losing whatever inheritance might still be theirs. The individual conflicts are rendered more intense by the lingering presence of the Survenant in the hearts of Angélina and Alphonsine especially—an ambivalent presence composed of humble thankfulness for the plenitude and joy he brought to them, of resentment for the pain and emptiness he inflicted upon them. Although the novel's second part ostensibly traces the development of Amable and Alphonsine's daughter, and her name, Marie-Didace, provides the book's title, the real subject is, in truth, the pathetic Alphonsine and her mediocre lot in life. Guèvremont carefully delineates the character's past to account for her present inability to cope with even her relatively uncomplicated village existence. Torn from her surroundings at an early age, saddled with a gnawing sense of shame, Alphonsine finds herself once again rejected—by her father-in-law for failing to provide a male heir—and abandoned—by the Survenant and by the death of her husband; confronted and beaten— by "l'Acayenne" in their struggle for domestic dominance. The diptych forms a regionalist novel in pretext only; its raison d'être is the pity and compassion for loneliness, the poetry and evanescence of solitude.

Gabrielle Roy (1909–1983)

In the novels under consideration Gabrielle Roy's foremost fictional preoccupation is the psychology of her characters; style, plot, and description are conceived in terms of and flow from the characterizations themselves. Her style has a forthrightness directly proportionate to her characters' willful reactions to inner emotions which they are forced to unscramble and outer situations with which they must deal. Roy uses her visually charged descriptive technique to localize her characters in a distinct physical and social milieu which explains their psychological being and extends it into tangible acts and concrete discourse. This precise, calculated description is one of the basics of Roy's fiction, for it serves to emphasize both the harsh reality facing her protagonists and, by opposition, a more peaceful, enriching ideal which they constantly, but vainly strive to attain. Contrary to the static presentation of characters all of a piece at the outset of the novel, common practice in nineteenth and early twentieth-century prose, Roy's characterizations are mobile and fluid, evolving in fragmentary fashion as the novel progresses. At times the character comes to us from the authorial viewpoint, Roy sketching out an individual physique and psyche. At other times she prefers an oblique technique, varying the viewpoints by elaborating a character's temperament and personality according to other characters' reactions and attitudes. At yet other moments, the reader is given direct access to the character when, through interior monologues, he reveals himself, tries to understand better and cope with himself and the world about him. Such a relativistic procedure gives the human elements of Royan fiction an elasticity, a sense of growth in time and space, a semblance of richness and contradictoriness up to then unknown in francophone Canadian writing.

Au pied de la pente douce and *Bonheur d'occasion (The Tin Flute)*, 1945, two urban novels, appeared within months of each other; though both are unanimist and populist, Roy's novel has none of the caricatural aspects that typify Lemelin's book. Montreal's Saint-Henri section is beset by unremitting poverty and misery, plagued by aborted individual revolts against a society gone awry which the Lacasse family and their ilk are powerless to understand, let alone control. They can at best grapple with their own personal problems in negative terms: Florentine's dejection enables her to overcome her ill-starred love for Jean Lévesque just enough to live in a wish-fulfillment world with Jean's surrogate, Emmanuel Letourneau. Rose-Anna's self-denial, which leads to emotional exhaustion, prevents the family's tottering to its fall while at the same time it locks Rose-Anna into her nostalgic world of youth and happiness. Azarius's naiveté and simplistic sentimentality ultimately allow him to enlist as a soldier, thereby affording a certain financial stability to what is left of his family. These are the deep-seated motivations that Roy's observational abilities seek to bring to the surface of her characters in a book that is far more brooding and pessimistic than most critics have been wont to consider it. Grief and anguish are but rarely and briefly counterbalanced by joy and peace.

The social reality in *Bonheur d'occasion* comprises what is seen as a necessary evil of mediocre existence: delusion and disillusionment. Poverty charts the lives of those who live in Saint-Henri, tainting them with the certitude of fatalism and only occasionally provoking a thwarted rebellion that is more an unstated acquiescence to the system than a real challenge to it. Saint-Henri can in fact be taken as the central protagonist of Roy's novel, the collective conscience of which the various characters offer outer manifestations. Jean Lévesque's is the only true revolt—ruthless and permanent—and, not insignificantly, Roy treats it episodically, perhaps hoping that the very mercilessness it incarnates and requires can be avoided in creating a more just and equitable society. When Jean brutally rejects Florentine, it is Saint-Henri that he rejects, its misery and hopelessness, a past marred by desperate solitude, a future doomed to pettiness. The other Lacasses and even the younger, theoretically more revolt-prone characters like Pitou, Alphonse, or Boisvert who congregate at mother Philibert's store or the Two Records bar offer no more than passive resistance or active subjection to events that are beyond the scope of their comprehension. Unable to change the course of those events or their own lot in life, they live as marginal beings faced with a war on another continent when their country is at peace, caught in an unemployment crisis (within what is, after all, a moneyed society), poverty-ridden while their anglophone neighbors in the Westmount section enjoy easy prosperity.

Whatever might be adumbrated at mother Philibert's or the Two Records bar by way of social revolt is limited to twaddle—there is no communal grievance at work nor any consciousness-raising to speak of. Lévesque remains the sole character to act upon his principles and act out his personal victory against mediocrity and futility. At most, the characters, including Azarius, who gather at these two favorite spots, indulge in fond hopes of an ideal postwar world and nurture a comforting but unproductive sense of community and fraternity in oppression. The social, economic, and educational horizons of Saint-Henri close in upon its inhabitants, despite or perhaps because of their weak and vaguely elucidated vision of themselves in a new society. Roy's world in this novel is such that its characters are and must continue to be in the image of their class and moment in history. Thus *Bonheur d'occasion* ends on the same tonality with which it began: the "immense weariness of life." The phrase is a leitmotif that runs throughout the work. As Emmanuel leaves Florentine for the war, the narrator's eye focuses on a tree, its branches twisted, its leaves dead before having had a chance to develop fully; in the threatening sky dark clouds herald an approaching storm.

For *La Petite Poule d'eau (Where Nests the Water Hen)*, 1950, Roy shifts from urban to rural geography, more exactly the wilderness of her native Manitoba where the Toussignant family live on an island in the river that gives its name to the novel. Although the locale has radically changed, certain key thematic preoccupations carry over from *Bonheur d'occasion*. If the wretched of Saint-Henri are overwhelmed by an anonymous industrial machine which renders them insignificant but integral parts of that machine, the Toussignants and their children are dwarfed into the boredom and routine of a living death by the immensity of the lakes and forests that isolate them from the rest of the world. Two themes implicit in *Bonheur d'occasion* are brought to the forefront in *La Petite Poule d'eau:* criticism of heedlessly large families and inadequate public education. The life of the Toussignants and the novel itself are structured around the annual ritualistic trip that Luzina must make to Sainte-Rose-du-Lac because of yet another pregnancy. When, upon the instigation of Luzina herself, the provincial government sets up a local school, the die is cast in the direction of progress for the children who leave to further their newfound education elsewhere, but at the ironic price of yet greater aloneness for the parents who remain behind in a vast lost land. As in her first novel, Roy here portrays characters caught up in a fatalistic web of solitude and helplessness, suffering their fate by way of wish-fulfillment and fantasizing, like Rose-Anna, Florentine, and Azarius. Luzina sublimates her loneliness by living and enduring the isolation of fictional personages she meets in an adventure novel about the North Pole. Again, Roy studies marginal beings, this time subjected to an unrelentingly merciless nature which makes them hapless prisoners of their geographic and economic isolation.

Alexandre Chenevert (The Cashier) 1954, is less the socially conscious novel that *Bonheur d'occasion* was and more the intimate portrait of an ill and aging bank teller, a portrait which paradoxically, however, goes beyond the topical dimensions of *Bonheur d'occasion* (war, unemployment, housing crisis) to attain a deeper universal resonance. Roy looks with compassion and understanding upon another in her gallery of the humble of the earth, ferreting out the cause of his failures and their effects on his mental processes and his social behavior. Like others of her protagonists, Chenevert is a prisoner of his own fears, doubts, and phantasms, lacking the intellectual acumen to comprehend his neuroses and work them out into a productive practical reality. Remaining always on the nearer edge of despair, he retains the resilient resignation, the persistent obstinacy typical of Royan characters as they struggle with their inner demons. As in *La Petite Poule d'eau,* Roy stresses the nefarious influence of daily boredom and monotony, and the danger of deluding oneself into a solution that consists of dwelling in daydreams and reverie. Chenevert remains wholly alone in his anguish, unable to verbalize it and open himself to others, whom he has banished for failing to live up to an abstract ideal of humanity that he has established as a yardstick for measuring others' worth in his life and to society. A brief excursion of solace into the Laurentian countryside and a stay in the hospital just before his death provide but a transitory resolution to Chenevert's inability to believe in an abiding moral and social meaning to one's passage on earth. His bitter disquietude prevails, as does his belief in the absurdity of the human condition.

Like Françoise in Marcel Proust's *A la recherche du temps perdu (Remembrance of Things Past),* Chenevert bewails the evils perpetrated on humanity at large and far away, but he is incapable of showing pity for the fellow humans around him. Anxiety preys upon him during repeated bouts with insomnia as he takes on the woes of the world, suffering from his lack of inner peace, assured that he stands alone in the intensity of the emotions occasioned by the human misery he reads about in newspapers or sees on film. Beset by the deadly, incessant pressures of mediocre modern city life, Chenevert, little by little, is gouged out by worsening psychosomatic ills. He heeds the demands of his doctor and seeks refuge in nature, only to find solitude a total absence of all things rather than a comforting meditative presence. After his return to the city, and terminally sick with cancer, Chenevert is adamant to the last in his refusal to bring himself to reconciliatory terms with social reality; he considers death the sole sincere act to be accomplished. Roy's protagonist, tormented by doubt though he is, does not have the clear awareness that he is indeed the victim of the gratuitous absurdity of existence.

La Montagne secrète (The Secret Mountain), 1961, is essentially an allegory of the life of the artist; its central character, Pierre is meant to be representative of all creative beings. At the same time, the work appears as a hymn of love for the beauties of northern Canada, from the Northwest to the Ungava, and for the attraction inherent in the solitary existence of the artist.

As the novel begins, Pierre, a lone wanderer who enjoys sketching the people and places he encounters, is still searching for a direction, a meaning to his existence. He dimly perceives the possibility of alternatives—founding a family, remaining with the friend with whom he spends two years trapping and fishing—but he is impelled ever onward toward a goal as yet unknown. Pierre then finds "his" mountain, high in the Ungava. By now his reputation has spread across northern Canada, where he is known both as "the Loner" and as "the Man with the magic pencil." The mountain represents his muse, the source of his greatest inspirations, but also the special, very personal message that he is to transmit to the world.

Having discovered his mission, Pierre struggles to perfect his art in Paris where, through the help of friends and benefactors, he has been sent to study. His natural genius for sketching, immediately apparent to others, provides no satisfaction to the artist himself, for his sole ambition is to be a great painter. So preoccupied by the pursuit of this dream that he neglects his health, Pierre dies at the book's close; a self-portrait is his only painting in which his technique has proved adequate to express the subject.

Much the same reflection might be made concerning the author's work in this novel, which succeeds far more in giving greater understanding of Roy the writer than in depicting the world of Pierre the artist. As in the latter's canvasses, the raw talent is everywhere evident, but the finished construct is uneven, imperfectly realized. The problems derive from several sources. First, passages narrating the difficulties and dangers of life in the northern wilderness are never adequately developed. The author tells, but fails to show that death hovers constantly in the background as an ever-imminent possibility; the reader's pulse never quickens when Steve is trapped by a sudden storm in the middle of a frozen lake, nor when Pierre's canoe is caught in rapids that allow the barest of escapes. These and other obstacles and dangers appear as only so many straw men, set up in order to fall without resistance.

Roy's attempt at stylistic elegance in this novel results, surprisingly, in passages of utter awkwardness. The rare instances of direct dialogue sometimes resort to literary tenses that would be out of character for any but the most pedantic academicians. There are too many omitted articles, too many literary inversions of subject and verb, overly self-conscious displacements of adverbs and adverbial phrases, an almost naive use of exclamations. Such calling attention to technique causes the flow of ideas to seem halting and unnatural. Yet the text does at times soar, and certain scenes could easily be anthologized as models of their kind. The protagonist's pursuit and killing of the old caribou is one such episode where Roy's particular strengths come to the fore. The physical action provides a mere framework for philosophical introspection on and psychological adaptation to some of the harshest aspects of nature.

Replete with comments on the essence of the artistic vocation and even on specific techniques for communicating through creative reproduction of reality, the novel presents in abundant detail Roy's *ars poetica*. And, as is usual in her writing, there is a liberal sprinkling of general maxim-type statements on life and the art of living. Taken as a whole, *La Montagne secrète* elaborates an idea of the author herself, diligently working to perfect her craft, concerned with the role of art in her own existence, even more interested in the good that it might accomplish in the lives of others. This portrait of the artist, rather than that of Pierre, gives the book its abiding interest.

La Route d'Altamont (The Road Past Altamont), 1966, a novel of initiation, recounts episodes from four periods in the life of Christine, a narrator who has many traits in common with Gabrielle Roy; much of what the heroine learns comes from her awareness of what her mother feels and experiences during these same times.

Part 1, "My All-Powerful Grandmother," begins when the six-year-old Christine visits her grandmother. She observes, without fully comprehending, the immense, no-longer-utilized talents of this remarkable woman, the encroaching loneliness of her life, her muted rebellion against God. Her health failing, the grandmother is eventually persuaded to live with the girl's family, where, shortly afterward, a stroke paralyzes her. Christine begins to fathom the mysteries of aging, death, and the value of human love and communication as she sees her mother caring for the now-helpless old woman and compares photographs made in the grandmother's youth with the dying creature before her eyes.

The lessons continue in part 2, "The Old Man and the Child," in which Christine, soon after the grandmother's death, meets the 84-year-old Mister Saint-Hilaire and they become fast friends. The only real action in this longest section of the work is a trip the two take together to Lake Winnipeg, an excursion that emphasizes and whets Christine's and her mother's desire for travel, for new, renewing experiences, for seeing and feeling and living the previously unknown. Through Saint-Hilaire, Christine gains other perceptions on the problems of aging, other attitudes toward death, and other appreciations for the satisfaction of living well and fully at every age.

Part 3, "The Move," narrates the heroine's ride with a mover, an incident that allows Christine insights into poverty and existences seemingly without hope. The wanderlust theme is further developed, and, as in the first two sections, the world of childhood with its enthusiasms, joys, and frustrations is masterfully evoked.

Part 4, "Altamont Road," finds the narrator as a young adult. Just as Christine examines her relation to her mother and to the Manitoba of her childhood, even so her mother meditates upon *her* feelings toward the dead grandmother and Quebec where she herself was born. The mother realizes that she is increasingly taking on characteristics of the grandmother, while Christine, precisely because of her longing to know the world which she shares with her mother, is forced to leave the latter in order to seek her own destiny as a human and as a writer. Abandoned, so to speak, by her daughter, the mother finds her greatest fulfillment through the daughter's life and accomplishments.

The novel is memorable for the sensitivity with which Roy delineates delicate human emotions. Studying conflicts and power struggles within the family unit, she underlines the extent to which it is possible for all opponents to be right. Christine's initiation into life and its secrets is able to occur when she takes her place in the procession of generations, assuming responsibility for her own fate, yet filled with gratitude for what she has received from those who preceded her.

There appeared in the 1940s a writers' movement (a very loose one) that eschewed the frontal attack on contemporary society, preferring instead an oblique offensive that took the form of the psychological novel. Robert Charbonneau, François Hertel (*Anatole Laplante, curieux homme* [Anatole Laplante, strange man] 1944), Pierre Baillargeon, André Giroux (*Au-delà des visages* [Beyond faces], 1948), and Robert Elie, its principal representatives, each in his own way chose to examine closely certain social, moral, or ideological dominants of a province that was undergoing fundamental metamorphoses in the very fabric of its customs, traditions, and goals. One novelistic component does, however, typify all of these writers: a protagonist who serves as a microcosmic unit of society, who is studied at a moment of paroxysm in his personal and social development, whose profoundest self becomes the matter and structure of these authors' novels.

Robert Charbonneau (1911–1967)

In *Connaissance du personnage* (Knowledge of characters), 1944, a seminal work for Quebec letters, Robert Charbonneau definitively refutes the ideological, moralizing prose that for so long had been called novelistic writing, claiming that the character (man) is the sole subject and object of the novel. It is the novelist's role and function to probe that which, in the human being, goes beyond intellectual grasp, remains outside the full scope of understanding. In his imagined reality, the novelist focuses upon man's concrete acts as extensions of his spiritual self—acts which are revelatory of both his inner truths and his rapports with Other. Charbonneau insists that the psychological analysis that must inform the novel is not a matter of total cerebral dissection which is, according to him, impossible, given the fluid, mobile nature of man. Characters can be approached only as elusive creatures, at given moments, in certain circumstances, and then only for the novelist to make them and the reader aware of the faulty human knowledge of self and others. Charbonneau's own novels are therefore not clinical case studies, nor intellectualized explanations of his characters' inner mechanisms, but rather efforts at bringing those inner workings to a manifest surface level in their complex interrelationships, their tropistic reciprocal influences in fragments of developing tension or crisis. For Charbonneau the core of the drama in the human conscience is always located in struggle: against self and others, against obstacles to satisfaction and happiness. The novel must be, but can only be, the beginning of an answer to basic questions asked about man; indeed it may well be no more than groping for formulations of those questions on the nature of the psyche. This notion is at the heart of Charbonneau's ambivalent, ambiguous novels, which provide the reader with tacit psychological directions but no presupposed theory nor definitive response that would close the inquiry that the novels first instigate. The omniscient author, the omnipresent authorial intervention disappear in Charbonneau's works as do moral stance and judgmental attitude. For him and for the reader, the truth of a fictional being is not appropriated whole from reality but is a created truth possessing its own analogous authenticity, and it is that authenticated simulacrum that the novel investigates.

Charbonneau's aesthetics are put to the test in *Ils posséderont la terre* (They shall inherit the earth), excerpts of which appeared serially in 1938, 1940, 1941; it was published as a book in 1941. An austere work not surprisingly divested of a readily identifiable social context, it is devoid of such other appurtenances as country and traditions, easy portraiture and armchair analysis. It is, in short, a novel that signals a rupture with the conventions of Quebec's novelistic past. Charbonneau, for one thing, deals with the theme of adolescence, a topic up to then untouched by the French novel of Quebec, choosing as his subjects two young friends, André Laroudan and Edward Wilding. Readers of the time expecting a well-made novel setting forth, developing, and clarifying the problem of adolescent egotism found instead a work that delved into the implied contradictions between individuality and responsibility. Laroudan and Wilding are both taken at a revelatory moment of crisis, that transition zone between childhood and adulthood which, in its very nature, is no longer fully the one nor yet entirely the other.

Charbonneau evokes the confused revolt and aggressiveness in his characters, the selfishness that manifests itself in violent, irrational reactions, but he avoids the facile pinpointing of root causes, the complete analysis of that basic insecurity in the characters' attempts at realizing what they view as their personal freedom. Wilding and Laroudan are like wild men swinging through the trees, not quite knowing where to land or even whether they should land. Stray impulses and unsettled needs lead them to miscalculate the means at their disposal for attaining goals that they impose upon themselves, provoking in turn a decimating anguish that makes of them uneasy strangers to any given situation. The stronger the will to appropriate, the larger the distance between what is desired and what is realized. The sense of belonging to a wider social dimension while retaining the security of being in one's own space and time will not occur until both characters have overcome the fears of freeing their individual selves and opening themselves to others. Whereas André and Edward never achieve this requisite state, two other adolescent figures do. Fernand and Jérôme, neither one of whom is a victim of the need to dominate, are able to give and receive love, and thus "inherit the earth." Charbonneau thereby undermines the idea that this reality, although rarified and privileged, is impossible.

Prisoners of themselves in good measure for being blind to the fact that they have themselves been instrumental in creating their isolation, André and Edward are also blind to the redeeming force that lies within them. The creative power of responsibility would finally release them from their world of self-absorption and arbitrary demands and allow them to accept and live the autonomy of sharing. For Charbonneau it is this giving of self and acceptance of Other that alone allows self-knowledge and communication—hence the question of freedom and moral obligation that underlies his entire novel and organizes its psychological approach. For that is what *Ils posséderont la terre* is: an approach and not an arrival. Charbonneau gradually leads us to his protagonists by noting, but not elucidating their defiant gestures, their defensive acts, their unexpectedly transparent or deliberately opaque words. In his insistence upon the contradictory, ambivalent aspect of human behavior Charbonneau has written what might appear to be a loosely structured novel; in fact it is highly structured in its composition, cogent and coherent in its terse concision. But it is a work that accords full significance to silence and absence, and by this technique offers an approximate impression of human psychology rather than a defined expression of it.

In *Les Désirs et les jours* (Desires and days), 1948, Charbonneau pursues the study articulated in *Ils posséderont la terre*, deepening his novelistic world as the work traces the life of Auguste Prieur from adolescence through adulthood. As he becomes exposed to the egotistical aims of others, he finds his own egotism increased by the shabby mediocrity that has settled upon his life; idealistic desires have turned into days of dissatisfaction. Memory here will, however, play a role that it did not for Laroudan and Wilding; it urges Prieur, at first subconsciously, to go beyond the monotony of an existence based on crass materialism and success in politics and profession. In his growing alienation from the world he himself has carved (out of both compromise and thirst for power and fame), he twists through memorial processes to loftier past visions abandoned along the way. Prieur wants the fulfillment and happiness—the peace—that would come from the knowledge that his acts and choices are in consonance with his noblest ideals. Charbonneau, as in his earlier novel, emphasizes the fundamental problem of freedom in his protagonist's making decisions that obviate delusion and disillusionment. Prieur will realize himself fully and freely only when, feeling unloved and dominated, he deliberately, honestly, goes out to others rather than retreating further into himself, when, like Laroudan and Wilding before him, he ceases to dominate and appropriate things and beings. Having experienced the paltriness of his life and a certain irrevocable solitude which it has brought him, Prieur recovers possession of what still remains of his authentic self and regains the love and friendship of his boyhood companion, Pierre Massenac. At the close of *Les Désirs et les jours* Charbonneau's protagonist knows a liberty that he has long sought, but that is not without the scars of human aloneness.

Pierre Baillargeon (1916–1967)

Pierre Baillargeon is one of those Quebec novelists who are only recently being reevaluated in their proper literary, historical context, and for the worth of their work per se. The eponymous hero of Baillargeon's first novel *Les Médisances de Claude Perrin* (The cynicism of Claude Perrin), 1945, is a not unfamiliar figure in contemporary fiction: a writer, alone and ill, alienated from society, desires, in a more natural solitude and in the further pursuit of writing, to bring a clearer meaning to his life and greater cohesion to his thoughts. The writer's awareness of his art is not without a close rapport with certain moral implications, for while Perrin is cynical in the abstract, he is ethically concerned in the concrete. Writing in the absence of any readers, Perrin considers that no one value system is any more meritorious than any other, but once the reader's presence asserts itself, it imposes upon writing a necessary sociomoral hierarchy. Baillargeon, as keenly taken by the state and evolution of francophone Canadian letters as Charbonneau, integrates into his novelistic world the principal personages that occupy literary time/space: author, narrator, character, reader, as well as the artistic means and human significance of writing.

In the pseudoautobiographical mode favored by a number of twentieth-century novelists, Perrin-Baillargeon discourses on himself, elaborating the links between a narrow personal scene and an overriding interest in Quebec literature on a "national" scale, as in the international standing of the province's writers. Perrin brings his intense gaze to bear upon the deepest levels of his psyche, and this close self-scrutiny of dashed hopes, of literary frustrations and unfound happiness, especially, colors his view of the world immediately about him. Baillargeon structures the entire novel around two subjective modes which account for the work's dual time frame. Perrin's quest for a fuller significance to his life and his need to write push the novel both back in time for a reevaluation of past failings and, simultaneously, forward in an appraisal of his potentiality and possibilities as a writer. The narrative levels, furthermore, slide from first to third person as the protagonist moves from past to present to future, from the awareness of a new individual self to the grasp of a wider sense of literary identity and commitment. It is characteristic of the psychological novel of the period that this nascent self evolves fully from within *Les Médisances de Claude Perrin,* and not according to predetermined conventions and formulas from without.

Just as Robert Charbonneau enlarges his novelistic universe from one book to another by developing certain recurring characters or situational spaces, so Baillargeon generates an ever deeper investigation into daily psychic reality by Claude Perrin's continuing first-person monologues in *Commerce* (Commerce), 1947. Perrin is a Montreal bookseller whose shop is an intellectual exchange place for ideas and attitudes, for paradoxical dialogues growing out of Perrin's personal ruminations and experiences—whence the book's title. An essentially solitary figure, Perrin struggles with the basic intellectual dichotomy that characterized his earlier incarnation—the obsessional give-and-take between the personal and impersonal, the abstract and the concrete, between compassion and indifference in his relationships with himself and others. Baillargeon imprints on his novel a spiral structure wherein the passage upward from the first to the second part is from a book about Perrin to a book by Perrin; though the merchant of ideas has not resolved his dilemma, the writer of maxims and epigrams has managed to exteriorize it by manipulating words. The art of writing is thus a redemptive act, a freeing power which makes of inner life, life itself.

Robert Elie (1915–1973)

Robert Elie's *La Fin des songes (Farewell My Dreams),* 1950, one of the darkest-hued among the psychological novels of the mid-1940s and early 1950s, studies its protagonist Marcel Larocque's steady disintegration to suicide as he helplessly fights to fend off the encroaching senselessness of life. Like other principal characters in these novels, Larocque is finely, incessantly tuned to the slightest advances and retreats of his psyche, hypersensitive to the multitude of phantasms that torment his mind. He is unlike the others, however, in that his metaphysical anxiety paralyzes him to the point of robbing him of all syntonic capability in his interpersonal environment. The quest for full authentic self and the certitude that such a complete discovery cannot ever be achieved gave to Charbonneau's and Baillargeon's characters their strength and a certain illumination; these same aspects of quest and certitude fire Larocque's despair and constitute his ultimate refutation of life.

Elie's character has, perhaps willfully, severed an indispensable link that would assure an adequate functioning in quotidian reality, and he thus remains mired in an ongoing silent monologue (i.e., which never attains the status of significant dialogue with others) that transforms others into enemies and negates life itself. Elie's text points clearly enough to the unhealthy nature of Larocque's introversion; aware of the emptiness that inhabits him, he seems bent on waging a struggle not to come to productive terms with the threatening void, hanging onto his comforting illusions instead, refusing life when it appears about to revivify the dead man within him. In the first part of the book's ternary structure Elie plunges the reader immediately into his character's full-blown depressive crisis; in the second part, titled "Marcel's Diary," the distanced third-person point of observation is abandoned to eliminate the intermediary narrator standing between character and reader. The diary serves to corroborate the characterial notations in the first part, specifically Larocque's pathological estrangement from reality and his sense of physical and mental incapacitation. Crippled in his ability to work within the reality that surrounds him, Larocque's self-deprecating attitude places him outside that reality which he can only confront with fear and contempt.

The theme of adolescence is not without importance in understanding Larocque's dilemma. What for Charbonneau's characters is a transitory stage of development, lived during adolescence itself and worked out in adulthood, is a permanent state for Elie's character. Unable to realize adolescent ideals of interpersonal relationships and unwilling to reconcile those ideals and adult compromises, Larocque's anguish assumes a tone of bitter cynicism and admits of death as its sole solution, the only deliverance. As desperate as he subconsciously feels it to be, the end of his life appears as the beginning of his dreams. Elie's novel stands as a powerful, disturbing study of an incurable emptiness within, necessarily calling to itself yet another emptiness that at best seems only less disconsolate.

1950–1984

The continuing urbanization movement in Quebec and the growing sophistication of the reading public bring to the novel new thematic preoccupations and an acceptance of a genre which, earlier, had been the object of religious and moralistic suspicion. Analytically, novels become more subtle and complex; formalistically, they show experiment and diversity, especially after the 1960s. Writers no longer view the novel as a necessary tool for extolling the rural life or religious beliefs, nor do they retain the realistic mold, as represented by the novels of Lemelin and Roy, for example. Considerably more aware of fictional techniques per se, novelists of this period use the written book as a battleground, pitting fiction against reality and consciously presenting that fiction as a careful technical reworking of reality. They metamorphose the real outer world through personal inner visions by way of characters' immersion in given social situations and their reactions to individual psychological dilemmas. Authors now blend inner and outer dimensions of the novelistic experience just as they blend differing writing modes and optical vantage points in the telling of a story. Narrational approaches multiply as novelists move away from the time-honored omniscient, omnipresent authorial manner; in the process the reader is brought in as co-creator of the novel rather than being considered its passive receptor.

Elements of the old morality tale mix with realistic-naturalistic aspects of the sociologically oriented novel and the personalized psychological narrative. There are, in addition, more important crosscurrents between poetry and the novel, as prose writing becomes more symbolic and imagistic. This increased aesthetic awareness is one of the most significant developments in post-1950s novels; the genre is now thought to be a laboratory for formalistic innovations of the most diverse sorts and no longer merely a carbon copy of socioreligious values and mores indigenous to Quebec. Concurrently, specific themes become the object of open attack: Church domination in matters of moral comportment; political oppression of Quebecers at the hands of anglophone-dominated business interests; the family as hallowed institution and core of social vitality. Novelists espouse love and sex as thematic material in a way that would have been inconceivable a mere ten or twenty years earlier.

Whereas, in nineteenth and early twentieth-century incarnations, the novel fully and clearly accounted for complex human problems on the basis of solidly entrenched sociomoral principles, post-1950s prose recognizes the fragmented, open-ended nature of the human condition. Novels take on the contours of tentative question and debate, not of definitive resolution. Time and space are treated in simultaneous or juxtapositional structural configurations that defy the tradition of linear Aristotelian chronology. First-person narration and interior monologue appear for the first time as renewing techniques which, importantly, revise the roles of the author, narrator, character, and reader, relativizing their presence in the novelistic construct.

Novelists of the period assume themes and situations, or extend them, beyond the confines of autochthonous Quebec limits: existential anguish and alienation, the lack of intercommunicability, the stress of inner psychic temporality within a larger outer social context, reasons for and implications of desperation as acted out in suicide and murder, the seemingly necessary contradictory, oppositional nature of the human creature unable to cope with conventionally imposed norms of social behavior. Because of this directly confrontational attitude and the importance given to the purely aesthetic transformational function of the novel, the well-worn themes of family life, happiness and love, geography and nature, gain a radically different tonality from what one had heretofore observed in the Quebec novelistic tradition. Novelists scrutinize the tenuous, questionable links between inner self and outer life, between a precarious psychological existence and a suspicious physical world. Hence the preponderance of characters who are studied as marginal beings in society, beings in an endless, often aimless or futile quest for their truly individual selfhood. The largely passive modality of earlier characterial vehicles now becomes an active, painful attempt at realization and survival in the urban jungle or the deadening boredom of rural life. Creative ingenuity and technical prowess in novel writing attain an urgency equal to and, in certain cases, greater than characterial and situational presentation. The novel in Quebec has ceased to be that of past history; it is instead the novel of the present and of a possible future.

Since the 1960s, the novel has undergone a profound reshaping process that has permanently altered the form and content of prose writings. Novelists question, and often refute, many of the conventional and traditional modes, values, and aims attributed to the genre, as they seek to renew and experiment with the written word. The movement (not in any organized sense of the term) is, however, more of a determined evolution than a revolution, in the same way that the "New Novel," spearheaded by Alain Robbe-Grillet and Nathalie Sarraute, is in France during the same period. Quebec novelists now give a far greater degree of autonomy to their characters, increased flexibility to time and space, and an ambivalent openness to the architecture of the novel, all of which stem from a precisely *controlled* freedom in the act of writing. As authors plunge more deeply into analyses of the subconscious, writing itself becomes more self-conscious and often stylized in a freewheeling baroque manner. Novelists become more acutely aware of their Quebecitude and stress the importance of language itself for cultural and ethnic survival. Native geography and nature continue to play an essential role in novels that frequently take the form of parable or fantasy-fable about a free land and a free people.

Unlike France where the "New Novel" was replete with would-be official oracles, there was in Quebec no corpus of theoretical writings, no manifesto of rules and regulations, no one writer to stand out as leader. Novels were then and remain, instead, a highly personalized and individualized means of expression, although novelists of the period were certainly aware of innovations taking place on the European continent. The "Parti pris" (set purpose) group was the only organization that might have attained herald status had it not been for its excessive postures in matters relating to Quebec speech. The journal *Parti pris,* founded in 1963, aimed at linking the "Quiet Revolution" in society and politics to a linguistic revolution in literature. The "Parti pris" group espoused the notion of Quebec as a free socialist state, completely separated from the Church. Literature was to be the prime vehicle by which this sociopolitical quest was to be pursued: in 1964 the "Parti pris" publishing house became a reality. Its authors focused upon the underprivileged and politicized their novels in order to effect social and economic reforms. The intellectuals and theorists of the group insisted, unfortunately, that such politically committed novels be written in joual (deformation of French *cheval,* horse) or Quebec patois, not so much to sing its praises as to expose it deliberately as a reflection of a people's loss of native language and the ethnic values of an entire society. The dialectics may have been noteworthy, but the practical result was to limit severely audience receptivity and to create resentment and confusion among the many not intimately familiar with the intentions of "Parti pris." As an aesthetics therefore the group's concepts never materialized extensively, although the socioethical undercurrents have flowed into a great number of Quebec novels of the last twenty years.

The so-called "Quiet Revolution" of 1960 signals the coming to power of a liberal party that stresses Lionel Groulx's old call to repossession of the land by Francophones. In literature, the theme is first and foremost stressed in the poet Gaston Miron's *Vie agonique (The Agonized Life)* and in Gilles Leclerc's *Journal d'un inquisiteur* (Diary of an inquisitor), both of which appeared in that pivotal year; the influence of the "Revolution" has been felt in Quebec since that time. Writers experience and attempt to express a collective consciousness reawakened by sociopolitical tendencies of the moment, Quebec's historical past now being viewed as a long ethnic death process that must at all costs be reversed. The novel, at last given its due importance and validity, emerges as one of the most potent tools for a people to act in full awareness of a colonial, Church-dominated past to be shed and of a new and different future to be created. Writers, be they novelists, poets, or essayists, regard the book as the medium for a confrontation, whatever guise it may take, between a society's still possible death or its possible freedom and autonomy. A host of major novels since the "Quiet Revolution" appear thus to have at their heart a certain apocalyptic essence in the links they establish between writing and history in Quebec.

André Langevin (1927–   )

In the vein of the earlier generation of psychological novelists, André Langevin's primordial theme is the alienation of characters who fall victim to faulty communication with others, who are unable to accept and understand in either human or divine terms the absurdity of suffering and the moral judgment against helpless innocence; hence an all-pervasive despair in Langevin's novels. Similarly also, he avoids imposing a subjective authorial viewpoint, preferring instead the objectivity that allows problems to be developed from within the character's own subjectivity. Langevin's protagonists thereby attain a greater autonomy than was the case in his predecessors' works. The anguish that Langevinian heroes experience stems from their being witness to others' suffering—the death of a child, the suicide of the beloved—and exacerbates a basic questioning of divine goodness and charity. In a more corrosive manner it also results from an indelible feeling of solitude and isolation prompted by the quasi-certitude that union of love or communication in friendship is impossible. Just as love among fellow humans is felt as ineffective or is refused as inadequate, so also Christian faith and justice, resignation and morality, fail in their goals or are rejected as hypocritical. Langevin's protagonists are thwarted in their every effort to succor others and in the process are further alienated morally and spiritually. This sense of irreconcilability on both profane and divine planes incites an individually and socially oriented revolt that is pathetically short-lived, for, on the one hand, those to whom help is offered refuse that help and find solace in death; on the other, the figures representing Christian values are either ineffectual in their beliefs or betray those very values and beliefs. In the absence of any hoped-for solidarity there is only the tormenting evidence of solitariness.

Langevin's terse, imagistic style aptly transcribes his protagonists' spastic, inner psychic convolutions; the compact, tense situations in his novels derive from the psychology of his characters, their violent acts accounted for by visceral obsessions over which they possess no control. When confrontation, though not exchange, occurs between characters, it is but an enfeebled prolongation of introverted dialogue with a despairing and often desperate self.

In *Evadé de la nuit* (Night escape), 1951, Langevin's first novel, Jean Cherteffe searches in vain to free himself from phantasms of his childhood and recent adolescent past. Being orphaned (an early traumatic source of solitude for several Langevinian characters), Cherteffe labors under the delusion that by rescuing an acquaintance from his alcoholism he will exorcise the image of his alcoholic father who had abandoned him in an orphanage. Cherteffe's revolt fails, for he errs in seeking his own authentic identity by imposing an essentially false identity upon another. Benoît, possessing a lucidity that Cherteffe's insecurity prevents him from attaining, undeceives the latter as he categorically tells him that he cannot mold others in a truth he himself does not believe. Benoît's suicide, following the death of his son, and his mistress Micheline's death in pregnancy destroy the last of Cherteffe's illusions. Langevin's underlying thesis in this double failure is that no communication is at hand that can afford the plenitude of self, no power of mind can be summoned to transcend certain human impossibilities that must be accepted as facts.

Cherteffe exemplifies the dialectics that will inhabit all of Langevin's protagonists: trapped in his prison, he is forced, by the very outside circumstances that he tries to manipulate, to admit the impotence of his "nocturnal escape." That is, neither he nor anyone else is capable of finding the means to end his inner night, for while he fervently desires to share a communicative happiness, he simultaneously closes off his exclusive universe to all intermediary forces. His will to construct an authentic existence is at the same time his will to dissemble his true motives and needs, hence a refusal of life that is, helplessly, of his own doing. In a tensional movement that recurs in other Langevin characters Cherteffe attempts to create a present by shedding an unwanted past, without realizing that the past leaves indelible marks that effectively prevent any stabilization of the personality. His insistence on reconciling rather than confronting inevitable contradictions in their inherent complexity produces a loss of any functioning contact with his immediate reality and leads Cherteffe to suicide.

The devastating psychic interferences of past and present that play so central a role in understanding Jean Cherteffe lie likewise at the heart of Madeleine Dubois's character in *Poussière sur la ville (Dust over the City)*, 1953. Married to Doctor Alain Dubois and implicitly expected to conform to middle-class values and codes of comportment, she lives in a small mining town where her working-class origins explicitly dictate her individual and social existence. It is this basic discrepancy in the time and temper of her life that causes the unbridgeable distance between her and her husband. It is not enough that Alain be aware of and, indeed, generously accept his wife's insatiable animal instinct, her need for living in the fullness of the instant, however insensate a form that need may take.

The question is one of possession and freedom; the gap between the two, the total lack of communication is not so much due to the difference in their backgrounds as it is to Madeleine's perception of

the difference between her own past and present situations brought
about by those conflicting backgrounds. For as long as Alain possesses her, she is not free; and her husband's pathetic gestures at
assuring possession (the symbolic value of such offerings as the
bracelet, necklace, and roses which he purchases out of desperation)
merely serve to further alienate and anger his wife. Langevin stresses
in these and all his characters the element of irrational panic that
drives them to acts of reconciliation and appeasement which inevitably short-circuit, provoking instants of revolt equally doomed to
failure because of their very irrationality. Alain's attempts to obliter-
ate his anguish and suppressed rage in drink heighten his feelings
of guilt and impotence; Madeleine's affair with a truck driver back-
fires thanks to the local priest's underhand work, and she consequently kills herself after failing to kill her lover. With the exception
of the unctuous Doctor Lafleur, believer in divine providence, and
the self-righteous parish priest, the city of Macklin, as collective
character and conscience, tacitly approves Madeleine's affair with
one of its own, and mercilessly condemns Alain for his cowardice
as a cuckold.

Langevin's use of first-person narrative throughout might be expected to give a unified perspective to the book; in fact, the technique ruptures that perspective, for the reader is dealing at least as
often with Madeleine's surrogate view of the world as with Alain's.
As *Poussière sur la ville* progresses, the husband tries, in vain, to see
and comprehend a hopeless situation through his wife's eyes; this
psychological ploy, which may not bring any deeper insight, and
certainly no reversal in the couple's estrangement, does result in
Alain's dogged persistence to remain in Macklin to redeem his wife's
death, perhaps even to atone for it, by gaining the city's respect
and confidence.

This split-vision, first-person narrative corresponding to a character's schizoid personality gives way to a plurality of viewpoints in
Le Temps des hommes (Man's reckoning), 1956. Langevin's adoption
of the third person, in effect, brings to the foreground his principal
characters in such a way as to accord each his autonomy as the author
recedes to a neutral referential point. Like Dubois in *Poussière sur la
ville,* Pierre Dupas witnesses the death of a child and revolts against
the senseless suffering inflicted upon the pure and innocent by a
God seemingly immune to charity and justice. Dupas's doubts on
the reasonableness and efficacy of divine goodness as well as his

disapproval of the clergy's flagrant, materialistic interests cause him to leave the priesthood and join a team of lumberjacks in Canada's northern forest lands. Although he has abandoned the practice of the Church's rites and rituals, his spiritual aim on earth remains firmly entrenched within him.

His desire to save souls is, however, counterbalanced by a new compassion that his experiences force on him. Questions of human failings, the ravages of love and jealousy, the shame of humiliation, the force of anguish and despair, present a reality that Dupas witnesses and comes to understand less in exclusively other-worldly terms and more on a perishable moral scale. Surrounded by simple-minded, opaque beings, Dupas's sense of mission is sharpened by a drama that unfolds about him and that exemplifies, for him, moral decay and spiritual emptiness. Laurier, enraged by his wife's infidelity, kills her lover and flees with Dupas as hostage—a willing hostage, for Dupas's profound wish is to withdraw Laurier from what he perceives to be the most nefarious consequences of his act, a hardened isolation and a refusal of repentance. The novelistic and psychological structure here is similar to that in *Evadé de la nuit:* both Benoît and Laurier refuse the help tendered by Cherteffe and Dupas, and their deaths seal the failure of effort at communication and shared destinies.

Le Temps des hommes is in fact no more a time for men than it is a time for God. In Langevin's pessimistic world both are rejected by a humanity that is crippled in its suffering and incapable of surmounting the despair and self-deprecation that invade it. Langevin's works are dramas of deprivation wherein his characters possess neither the belief in God nor the faith in fellow humans that would enable them to cope better with an unconstrained absurdity. In their destitute condition they look with suspicion upon plenitude and good, just as they hold as inescapable fact egotism and evil. For Langevin, human relationships appear to be possible only at a distance, tenuously entertained by beings who, out of fear or pride, cannot or do not want to understand and thus exist in a self-fulfilling prophecy of fatalism.

Yves Thériault (1915–1983)

Yves Thériault is one of the most prolific of Quebec novelists; regrettably, prolixity does not assure quality of writing. *Aaron*

(Aaron), 1954, *Agaguk (Agaguk)*, 1958, and *Cul-de-sac (Cul-de-Sac)*, 1961, are perhaps his best works. Thériault employs a wide range of geographic cadres from metroplitan Montreal to rural villages to the wilds of Labrador and the Ungava. His literary space is filled with characters of varied ethnic origins, oppressed in some vital way, who emerge as the proponents or the victims of the liberation process. His Jewish, Indian, Eskimo, immigrant figures are most often rugged individualists living by the power of their instinctive beliefs and emotions in their struggle against totalitarian forces, whether these be social, moral, or religious in nature. This elemental movement in Thériault's characters, usually expressed as sexuality or physical or psychological violence, forms the basis for the author's vehement criticism of society and its institutions, which are seen as inhibiting the full realization of the authentic self. Thériault's literature of commitment attacks the legal, moral, and traditional repression of the individual, those restrictive aspects of the human community which isolate and alienate beings who are different, in favor of those who quietly assimilate.

The breadth of Thériault's novelistic techniques matches the diversity of geographic space and characterial ethnicity. In the earlier novels the style is of a popular turn, incorporating many Canadianisms; in a work such as *Aaron*, the style is, by contrast, excoriated, and picturesque description gives way to psychological introspection. Earlier works are furthermore written in the omniscient third-person narrative mode, whereas later novels, such as *Cul-de-sac*, use a more narrow, immediate, first-person narration.

Aaron centers on the differing social, moral, and religious attitudes and values that pit Moishe, representing strict Jewish orthodoxy, against his grandson Aaron, who revolts and rejects the mysticism and ancestral tradition in which he has been raised. Essentially, Thériault's novel is a penetrating study of the causes and effects of persecution: Moishe persecuted in the very roots of his being by a modern changing universe, symbolized by Aaron; Aaron persecuted by sanctions imposed from without, seemingly unjustified and existing as though in a void. It is also a novel of deliverance, as Thériault locates his two protagonists in worlds diametrically opposed and between which no communication exists. Moishe must, above all, save the religious vision which is his only reason for living; Aaron wishes to free himself from the misery and servitude of the Montreal slum existence which he has always known.

Aaron is anchored in a verifiable, contemporary realism as much as it is in an intense mysticism of immemorial dimensions. On another interpretational level, the old Jew's destiny can be equated to the Quebecer's: a persistent passive adherence to a past that is held as sacrosanct and, in consequence, the failure to integrate with an irreversible social evolution. But Aaron's lot is also the Quebecer's: he changes his name, renounces his ethnic heritage, and relinquishes his identity in a gesture of submission to the materialistic anglophone rulers.

Beyond religious and nationalist concerns *Aaron* is a forceful statement against the evils of intolerance in the context of North American society, for Aaron's vulnerability and revolt are in good part accounted for by his being the butt of his Gentile neighbors' racism. Choosing an ethnic setting not previously found in the Quebec novel, Thériault develops one of the very basic themes in all Quebec literature, that of possession and dispossession, autonomy and submission, difference and similitude. His protagonist is forced to act and react in full consciousness of his deeds and their consequences. Whether it be violently rejecting religious fanaticism, experiencing the pain inflicted by bigotry, or confronting present social reality, Aaron must deal with the fundamental problem of either accepting an externally imposed identity or, conversely, freely creating his own.

Despite widely divergent geographic settings—urban Montreal and the untamed Canadian tundra—there are striking thematic similarities between *Aaron* and *Agaguk*. The eponymous hero of the more recent novel overcomes the weight of Eskimo tribal traditionalism. Agaguk comes to know the solitude of a fanatic moral and social group and escapes from it toward a fuller sense of individuality and greater self-respect, thanks to the intervention of Iriook, his wife (a role played by the emancipated Jewess Viedna in *Aaron*). The character's growing isolation from his social unit is compounded by the alienation stemming from a white anglophone society which exploits the Eskimo in fur and animal trading. The book's dynamics are thus composed of the conflicts between the protagonist and a humanizing feminine presence, that is, between him and his ancestral society on one hand, and the ruling Canadian society on the other—and the partial resolution of those conflicts. In this regard, the ultimate act of Agaguk's liberation (and Iriook's influence) consists of his rejection of tribal rites in sparing his new-born child who is a daughter; the moral transcendence that Agaguk is able to accomplish by refusing to kill stands, furthermore, as an expiation for his earlier murder of a white trader. Thériault's novel can be read on one plane as sociological reportage on a marginal society within a society, on another plane as a psychological study of a character's evolution from instinctive violence to measured peace.

The work also, significantly, centers on the evolution of its female character, Iriook, who breaks with atavistic tribal customs by speaking out in support of her husband, by asserting her own autonomous self against both the tribe in general and Agaguk specifically. The author underscores the strength and courage that Iriook possesses, and that Agaguk receives only through her, by stressing her native introspection in dealing with the metamorphoses that will affect their present and future lives. Thériault makes it clear that Iriook is aware of the experience of deliverance in a way that Agaguk is not. Unable willingly to perceive Iriook as a free individual, Agaguk is forced by her words and actions to recognize her difference as other than an inferior member of the tribe. Typically for Thériault's characters, Iriook attains her liberty through an experience of alienation. Perhaps never before in the Quebec novel has a female character had the status that she achieves in *Agaguk*.

Cul-de-sac, on the other hand, shows not a winner but a victim in the struggle for liberation. In truth, Victor Debreux can hardly be said to resist the oppression that he clearly recognizes. Condemning all-inclusively the bourgeois milieu from which he comes— not merely its smugness, its overriding concern with public opinion, its prejudices, gossip, basic selfishness, and emptiness of any genuine impulse toward generosity, hope, or love, but also, because of his own stubbornly predetermined negativism, its every attitude that, to a less biased observer, would represent virtues and strengths— he weakly acquiesces to the roles assigned him by his family and society. His acts of rebellion are two: first, he seeks self-destruction through alcoholism. Second, he narrates this text, a groveling confession which, were it successful, would condemn all society, implicate the reader directly, and, though perhaps not justify the narrator, at least prove that he is as worthy as anyone else.

Technical problems mar the novel's total effectiveness. The principal structuring device—Debreux's falling over a precipice, being unable to move, remembering the major events of his life—seems too consciously symbolic, arbitrary, contrived. Certain plot elements lack verisimilitude. It seems highly unlikely that a single conversation, no matter what truths it might reveal, would catalyze the immediate change of a person who had never before been drunk into a constantly excessive drinker. Nor does it appear realistic that an engineer whose previous work experience was limited to verifying the calculations of his seniors would, after losing his position and undergoing treatment for alcoholism, be given immediately thereafter a job on which he was responsible for twelve other engineers and a thousand laborers.

Secondary characters, which is to say everyone except the narrator, exist only as types, not as individuals. Some, such as the father or the senior partners in the engineering firm, are mere caricatures. Fabienne, Debreux's great love, provides a pat, though improbable contrast with all the others; she is conveniently disposed of in an automobile accident.

The virtues of this novel lie in its often-devastating satire of bourgeois banality. Landscapes, their beauties and their hidden menaces, are evoked with the sure craft of an expert writer. Moreover, Victor Debreux stands out as a masterfully developed character, whose self-pity and self-indulgence, presented under the guise of self-recrimination, make him one of the least likable in all Quebec literature.

Anne Hébert (1916–)

Anne Hébert has, since the start of her career, been one of Quebec's outstanding writers, attaining international recognition as both poet and novelist. In *Les Chambres de bois (The Silent Rooms)*, 1958, her first novel, Hébert explores a multifaceted dreamlike world of anguish and evil not dissimilar to the universe of her poetry. Eschewing both the realistic and psychological novel traditions, she infuses her prose with a poetic resonance that is new to the genre in Quebec. Catherine, the principal character, upon her marriage to Michel, finds herself face to face with a husband obsessed with his childhood and tormented by the absence of his sister Lia for whom he feels a quasi-incestuous love. In the limited space of their two Parisian rooms Catherine dwells mostly in the limitless time forced upon her by the wall of separation from her husband, whose identification with his past is as certain as Catherine's own present becomes ever more insecure. The immobility and silence that dominate the relationship is broken by Lia's return, but only to further exclude Catherine, as Michel and his sister again re-create their exclusive, but untamed Edenic existence. The life force in Catherine is strong enough for her to break away from the nocturnal bonds of the rooms and flee the city. The movement is a constant in Hébert's novelistic world: a determined flight from the grip of death (here Michel and Lia's frozen state of pre-adulthood) toward a struggle for life and truth, from condemnation to salvation.

By and large, Catherine functions as observer of the situation in which she is a passive agent until Lia's return. Temporally and spatially, *Les Chambres de bois*'s architecture is one of passage from past to present to future, coinciding with Catherine's possession of self, loss of that self-possession, and regaining of self-identity. The character's psychology, as so often in Quebec novels, also coincides with the historical themes of possession and dispossession of land and country under anglophone authority. Catherine, dispossessed in the silent rooms, becomes a mere object to be manipulated according to Michel's (and Lia's) domineering whims and wills. The year of publication is 1958 and rumblings of the "Quiet Revolution" can already be heard as the old French Canadian mold is inexorably shaping into new Quebec selfhood. Just as Catherine lived for and by herself before her marriage with (and subjugation to) Michel and wills to do the same when she chooses to leave him, so also is French Canada's historicity a movement from French self-rule to English domination and, after 1960, toward a renewed affirmation of native ethnic identity. Catherine/Quebec no longer accepts her lot as a passive plaything of an authoritarian ruler, but seeks out her freedom and autonomy as a human being in her own right.

Hébert's protagonist, from her observational point, spins out the web of analogies that build up in her, intermeshing notations on the rooms' physicality (their oppressive presence, their eerie menace) and on Michel's intractable psychological behavior (his brooding silence, his fascination with immobility and death). Although the novel is constructed with carefully detailed descriptions, it never falls into the analytical mode, but rather suggests moods provoked by the physical and psychical atmosphere that surrounds and impinges upon Catherine. Hébert refrains (most of the time) from interpolating authorial comments, explanations, or judgments, preferring instead a poeticized evocation of sensations as they become consciously significant to her heroine: this significance resides more in feeling than in speech, in quiet observation more than in vivid imagination. Reality merely presents itself to Catherine's awareness; and after roaming in obscure regions of her psyche, it finally surges to the surface in her decision to free herself from her oppressors. In sketching out the book's ambience and her character's mental and emotional mechanisms, Hébert successfully, and for the first time in Quebec, fuses poetry to the novel. The technique will not fail to be influential on future novelistic production.

In *Kamouraska (Kamouraska)*, 1970, Hébert pursues her investigation of a world haunted by guilt and innocence, hope and despair, violence and inertia. Elisabeth d'Aulnières, raised by three celibate aunts according to a strict and restrictive code of moral order and social behavior, is married to an unbridled tyrant, Antoine de Tassy. Humiliated and oppressed, Elisabeth subsequently falls in love with an American doctor, Georges Nelson, whom she persuades to kill her husband, only to reject Nelson for the act he commits at her instigation. The ambivalence that dominates *Kamouraska* revolves mainly about the discrepancy between what the protagonist knows and understands about herself and those around her, and what she thinks she knows and understands. Elisabeth lives as a marginal being in a futile universe, accomplishing daily ritualistic gestures to mask over the emptiness and inevitable joylessness of her existence. The (anti-)heroine's desperate move to have her husband killed only serves to provoke an agonizing inner confrontation between the truth and the lie of her self. As elsewhere in Hébert's works, the dialectical tension here ultimately points up the lie, but also the fathomlessness of truth in the character's mind.

Elisabeth's attempts to unravel her past bring with them both fear and fascination, for she at once denounces the inauthenticity of her present life and yet is unable to face the authenticity of her past motivations and actions. Hébert architects *Kamouraska* upon this implacable movement back in time from a fixed point in the present— the past composed of tripartite panels encompassing Elisabeth's childhood-adolescence, her marriage with Tassy, and her affair with Nelson; the present, the eighteen-year time unit of conjugal life with the mediocre Jérôme Rolland. In the gradual, if partial, self-revelation or confession that comprises the entire book the reader comes to understand, however obliquely, what escapes the character herself: the basic unresolvable duality that inhabits Elisabeth. She is a woman who, compulsively, needs a sense of order, virtue, and social honor, but who incarnates fundamental feelings of vengeance and evil. The book's interrogation focuses on the psychological nature of this rupture of self and on the implications of these contradictory forces outside one's control and comprehension, forces that effectively prevent bridging the gulf between oneself and the outer world. Confrontation does not lead to reconciliation but to greater divisiveness.

Kamouraska represents a long, arduous journey through memory, the present existing only in anticipation of a past that Elisabeth (re-)invents as her examination reveals it to her. The work is thus also a voyage through dream and imagination, to which Elisabeth ascribes a liberating function as she seeks to understand and accept the duality that informs her whole being. What Hébert underscores is that, in fact, memory and imagination are inescapably linked, that the past is trapped in the memory, that her heroine cannot but remain imprisoned in the irreducible contradictions brought about by a set social, moral, and religious education. Defenseless against the memorial process, Elisabeth is alone in her psychic exile; desirous of a metamorphosis from mask to true visage, she plunges into an oneiric time and space, escaping into her past at the same time that she flees from it. Hébert entraps the protagonist into her dilemma by a nefarious network of obsessive images: water and fire, mud and snow, blood and thirst. Significantly, Elisabeth weaves a red flower into a tapestry as Nelson heads north for the appointed murder; slowly and inevitably the shift is made from the woven woolen flower to the red "flower" of blood and death in the virgin snow. With the murder of Tassy, Elisabeth's sense of moral virginity has again been tainted and she is free—or rather, destined—to accuse and reject her lover as being solely responsible for the evil perpetrated, as she had earlier accused and rejected her husband, and the servant Aurélie Caron as true instigator of Elisabeth's affair with Nelson and of Tassy's murder.

Herein lies the essence of Elisabeth's dilemma and of Hébert's sociomoral criticism inherent throughout *Kamouraska:* the religious tenet that preaches that flesh is sin, an evil to be rooted out, avoided, or worse, repressed. Hence the author chooses a character irreparably torn between two unbridgeable moral systems: virtue and abstinence, symbolized by Elisabeth's three aunts; and desire and sex, symbolized by Aurélie, the "sorceress." Hence also the entire novel— the reconstruction of the crime and the trial—is presented as a study of Elisabeth's split personality, of Elisabeth and Aurélie as doubles. Desire is thus portrayed, imagistically and psychologically, as a dark, obscure force that sullies and destroys, that pushes aggression to brutal violence. It attains the status of an uncontrollable, magical, mythical power which seizes Elisabeth; it is, furthermore, associated in Antoine with the death-wish, that is, an understated need for expiation.

In her novel Hébert evokes, in poetically powerful fashion, a society that condemns more than it condones and does so on absolute religious terms incompatible with human needs and failings. *Kamouraska*'s trenchant closing image best expresses Hébert's denunciation of a society that dispossesses its members of their authentic individual selves: a woman in black is exhumed, alive, and roams the land out of a desire to live, a right to live, only to be left to die once again in total solitude and exile.

Violence and revolt are again in the forefront in *Les Enfants du sabbat (Children of the Black Sabbath)*, 1975, as the novel's protagonist, Sister Julie, falls prey to an invidious hallucinatory introversion. Hébert associates the Catholic ceremonial with the black rituals of sorcery, portraying Sister Julie as a novice become victim in the religious order of the Precious Blood. Innocence comes to grips with persecution when she attempts to heed the call to life and freedom against the will to persevere in sacrifice and atonement. Under yet another, and this time more totalitarian disguise, Hébert elaborates the typography and mythology of Quebec in a novel that makes strong social and moral claims.

The very beginning states the principal character's intention to rid herself of destructive obsessions by a necessary exorcism of her personal demons, and in its circular construction the book closes with the heroine's escape from the convent grave. As opposed to Elisabeth's final alienation in *Kamouraska*, Sister Julie realizes her liberation. Significantly, the passage from condemnation to freedom of self is not by way of expiation for supposed sin, nor a sublimation of feelings of guilt. Hébert, on the contrary, utilizes her characters as a vehicle for denouncing the long tradition of imposed guilt on the Quebec soul. Sister Julie/country refuses a comportment tainted by feelings of prison and death which her very nature finds untenable, and opts instead for her authenticity and autonomy.

The authoritarian figures of the three aunts in *Kamouraska* find their counterparts here in the convent's Mother Superior and her colleagues. For these there exists a Manichaean world of Good and Evil, severe religious principles composing the first, the other encompassing all of lay life. God inhabits the convent, the devil dwells in the world, hence Mother Marie-Clothilde's seeing in Sister Julie the devil's surrogate. The novice's anguishing need to live the plenitude of life is translated by the Mother Superior as a diabolical desire for sin and lust. In the two characters Hébert confronts two antagonistic forces: a life restricted and ruled by absolute religious dogma, and a life free of the Catholic teachings that have so long held Quebec prisoner. For the one, intolerable evil resides in the very desire to live one's free life based upon larger ethical considerations; for the other, the life of blind unquestioning worship represents an unnatural order of things. The novel as a whole takes on the form of an epic, mythic, life-and-death battle waged on Quebec terrain. And though the death of Sister Julie's child (Satan's offspring) at the Mother Superior's hands conveys an impression of victory for the religious code, it is Sister Julie's espousal of a more humanistic moral order that is the veritable triumph in *Les Enfants du sabbat*.

Hébert, more overtly and forcefully than ever before, attacks taboo subjects ingrained in the Quebec moral fabric: the sense of shame cultivated by the Church, the false sense of security in religious faith, the cult of hope in death and the beyond (most vividly symbolized here as in *Kamouraska* by the figure of the black-robed woman). The mystical life (or more precisely the mystico-erotic life) is a scene of cruelty and horror, of hellish, terror-ridden phantasms. The author pointedly depicts the cloistral existence as a symbol of society's equation of passion and lust with death, its blind virtuousness, if not uncompromising idolatry, a folly and source of oppression that Hébert hopes to exorcise in her reader by means of its excessive and monstrous incarnation. By her poeticized images, symbols, and themes Hébert offers a liberating rite, a healthy aggressivity to counterbalance a ubiquitous inferiority syndrome. As in her other works, one finds Quebec at the very heart of her vision of the world, a translucent vision that seeks above all to reshape Quebec identity by exposing a part of its soul which has been too long passed over in silence.

After the novella *Héloïse* (1980), in which Paris figured as the locale, *Les Fous de Bassan (In the Shadow of the Wind)*, 1982, signals Hébert's return to Quebec as a backdrop for her study of the solitude and alienation of beings caught up in a web of desire and violence. Hébert's view of the universe manifests itself once again in situations and characters whose dual nature reveals intense good and evil, love and hate, compassion and vengefulness. In a now-familiar but ever-renewing Hébertian scenario, sensual/sexual obsessions and their inevitable composites of inner fear and fascination take the outer forms of domination and death, or suffering and silence, or submission and dispossession. Here the author assigns destructive power to male characters, humiliation to female characters, but suppressed passions and overwhelming feelings of guilt and discontent haunt all of them. A brooding pessimism, a sense of helplessness and hopelessness, invades the entire book, in which characters seek havens of peace whereas none can exist, or concoct cosmologies to fill the voids left by daily reality.

Like *Kamouraska* and *Les Enfants du sabbat,* especially, *Les Fous de Bassan* is a tensely dramatic work, carefully controlled in structure, and combining, in its descriptions and serial monologues, the realistic and the poetic to compose a disquieting mythology of past and present as characters attempt in turn to reconstruct and come to terms with traumatic events in their lives. The novel's ambivalence resides in these characters' constant seesaw between the expressed and the repressed, fact and phantasm, faced as they are with their own instability and the chaos of the world about them. For them, life appears as an exercise in ultimate powerlessness and disintegration, an existence lived in fleeting images of a threatening imminence rather than in any secure state of immanence.

Hébert chooses an anglophone setting for this novel: a community descended from English loyalists who, in the late eighteenth century, emigrated to Quebec rather than remain in the United States and be forced to become American citizens. The drama unfolds during the summer of 1936 in the imaginary village of Griffin Creek, isolated from other Protestant anglophone communities and turned in upon its tortured anguish. Where in *Kamouraska* snow and cold were of paramount importance in character development, here the sea and the wind exert a quasi-evil, magical influence, notably upon Nora Atkins and Stevens Brown in their story of desire and death. Under the claustrophobic weight and threat of a stark nature and austere society, five characters present variant versions of the fateful summer of 1936 and in particular of the night of 31 August, shrouded in mystery and awe, the night of Nora's and her cousin

Olivia's death. Using interior monologues, epistolary and diary forms, and multiple-narrative technique, Hébert divides her novel into six segments, each of which, though it has its own narrative voice, is imbued with a distinctly Hébertian poetic timbre. The author frames her work within the same distanced, ironic focus that she used in *Kamouraska;* in this case, Reverend Nicolas Jones and Stevens Brown (the [supposed] murderer—critics have been too hasty in their assumption of his guilt, for the book simply does not provide sufficient conclusive evidence on this point), at a remove of forty-six years, recount the tale as each recalls it. Dated "Autumn 1982" and titled "The Book of Reverend Nicolas Jones" and "Last Letter from Stevens Brown to Michael Hotchkiss," these opening and closing fragments of the narration strike the reader rather as a same omnipresent authorial voice and not differing narratorial ones (the work's publication date, is, coincidentally, September 1982). Within this temporal and vocal frame the author's eye penetrates to "summer 1936" itself for fragments two, three, and four, respectively, "Letters from Stevens Brown to Michael Hotchkiss," "The Book of Nora Atkins," and "The Book of Perceval Brown and of Some Others." The penultimate section, significantly for the work's poetic and cosmic dimensions, bears the notation "no date" and thus extends outside of time. It is limited by no epistolary or novelistic genre, titled simply "Olivia of the High Seas." Furthermore, this fifth fragment's narrative "I," ostensibly Olivia, tells her story of Griffin Creek as viewed *after* her death, as the opening sentence makes clear. Perhaps more than in any other of Hébert's works (save *Héloïse?*), lines of demarcation between the real and the imagined, uncontrolled obsession and lucid rationality, blur in and out of each other. Not surprisingly, therefore, in this tense and dense novel the richest poetic aura is given to the book of Perceval Brown—Perceval (Stevens's brother and other self who refutes Stevens's [alleged] crime as imposture and mockery), the "idiot," but in whose wisdom and tenderness and far-seeing vision reside some quintessential Hébertian values concerning human inadequacies and possibilities.

In *Les Fous de Bassan* Hébert, more deeply yet, examines the psychic workings of passion and imagination, seemingly under the spell of fatal laws that blind or goad their victims into crippling impasses or provocative and largely (self-)destructive acts. Obsessive multiple-sense imagery (piercing sounds, oppressive colors, painful odors) and the loss of childhood as a recurrent theme, both of which are ascribed especially to the female characters, stress once again Hébert's fundamental feminist preoccupations. These preoccupations too, however, are bathed in ambivalence (witness, e.g., the earlier cases of Catherine in *Les Chambres de bois* and of Elisabeth in *Kamouraska:* the line between the protagonist's condonation and condemnation is slim and obscure) though the female figure as the object of oppression and suppression at the hands of the male appears more forthrightly set in this novel than in previous ones. Whether in fact or phantasm, Nora and Olivia seem doomed—in a sense punished—by the male who fears their very femininity and their assertion of it. What is certain, however, is that they symbolize a kind of primeval innocence which, given history and society, cannot exist, in the Hébertian context, except in a before-life (Nora's memory recalls a prior existence within the sea) and the afterlife (Olivia's memorial monologue is subsequent to her death). Between these two poles, the quest for domination and the recourse to vengeance, whether instigated by male or female, lead only to mutism, despair, and impotence.

Gérard Bessette (1920–)

Le Libraire (Not for Every Eye), 1960, is written in the form of a diary kept by the main character, Hervé Jodoin, a bookseller who lives in Saint-Joachim, a small Quebec town. Put in charge of the bookstore's stock of volumes on the Church's list of prohibited reading matter, Jodoin comes face to face with the town's pettiness and prejudices, as with the Church's censorship practices. Having lost all illusions and harboring precious little ambition, Jodoin laconically accepts the world's shortcomings with a general sense of contempt for humanity as a whole, and seeks only to be left in peace and tranquillity.

Le Libraire, one of those books written during the formative years of the "Quiet Revolution," appeared precisely in the 1960 landmark year. It also presents the narrative "I" as a sort of collective "we," the protagonist being both character and narrator, though his diary is penned a posteriori; that is, (virtually) every Sunday Jodoin inscribes the events of the preceding week. Bessette's underlining of the repressed element in society (Saint-Joachim's citizens very much want to read the condemned books but are afraid to do so) and the nefarious repressive cause (the Church's dominant moral role) are in

tandem with the ideological movement that calls for Quebec's socioeconomic autonomy and its freedom from the Church. But it is,
after all, a "quiet" revolution; the liberal party, in other words, the
upper bourgeoisie, wants control of the social machinery but is not
intent on sharing that control with the proletariat. Jodoin's insu-
larity from the populace, which he considers the incarnation of
stupidity and mediocrity, singularly echoes the social tendencies of
the time. Astute, gifted with a cunning sense of organizational
power, Jodoin analyzes and synthesizes reality according to his needs
and desires. He may appear to be a helpless drifter, a loner living
a marginal social existence; in fact, he has deliberately left an educational system that he evidently considered antiquated and stifling, preferring instead to fashion a mode of life to his own personal
advantage, as "quiet" as it may seem. Again, the larger social
parallelism stands out clearly enough: in 1960 a social class takes
over power in order to transform to its own advantage the socioeconomic and political fabric of Quebec.

Jodoin's diary (Bessette's novel) proceeds in as precise and tightly
controlled a manner as Jodoin's actions and reactions in the various
situations that challenge him. His rigorously synchronized private
writing is the formal counterpart of his analytical acumen in dealing
with the importunate public that he characterizes as "disgusting
questioner." In a way reminiscent of Samuel Beckett's characters,
Jodoin seems bent above all on avoiding speech and movement, and
the bookstore becomes a refuge of silence, his room a haven for
writing, the local tavern a place of solitude in drink. But if Jodoin
is sparing in the spoken word, he is generous in the written word,
appropriating the world surrounding him by a kind of "quiet"
conquest that is revelatory of his own sociopsychological substance
as well as of relationships (if one can go so far as to call them that),
such as he envisions them, with others. Bessette accords his protagonist a striking mixture of very familiar, popular speech and
studied, mannered turns of phrase, with the aim of stressing Jodoin's
irony and downright sarcasm concerning his fellowmen. In this
respect, writing comes across as a necessary safety valve for Jodoin's
excessive cynicism, aggressivity, and pent-up hostility. Similarly,
his acquaintance with and responsibility for the banned books release
energy reserves in him and increase his despotic dominance of his
clients, including the local parish priest when the latter officially
complains to Jodoin of the sale of one of those volumes.

Release resides, now, in the ability to calculate his spoken word as craftily as he does his diary discourse: Jodoin, the Quebecer, effects the passage from silence and idleness to speech and action. Ultimately, he will leave Saint-Joachim, and in Montreal will abandon the diary; it no longer is a necessary tool for the verbalization of his and society's ills. But the three-month Saint Joachim interval will have served as an apprenticeship in defiance and combativeness against Jodoin's passivity and what he perceives to be his fellow beings' lack of intellectual curiosity, their inability, or refusal, to realize their autonomy, from fear of long-standing moral and religious taboos. Rather than continue to see others as a threat to his very person and consequently withdraw into solitude and refute communication, Jodoin will assume his self through expropriation of his own valid speech. Bessette's novel, by means of a minutely contrived narrative mechanism, espouses the self-affirmation of a rejuvenated Quebec society's belief in its power and necessity. Bessette, here and elsewhere, conceives of literature as a liberating force, an evolutionary process that brings to the conscious level primordial human desires and requirements and then allows these to be satisfied and met.

Like *Le Libraire*, *L'Incubation (Incubation)*, 1965, has the trappings of a traditional tale (sexuality, jealousy, guilt, adultery); as in the earlier work the setting is realistically depicted: London, Montreal, and the university community of Narcotown. But this time Bessette takes giant steps toward technical virtuosity (though it is pallid here compared with that of *Les Anthropoïdes*) and toward more probing analysis of his characters' psyches. The entire narrative is in the form of stream-of-consciousness, with the flow of thoughts and emotions unimpeded by conventional punctuation. The strict and sustained application of this technique, new to the Quebec novel, plunges the reader immediately into the narrator Lagarde's awareness and into the lives of the key characters. The tenseness of the form is in precise chronometry with the intensity of the drama that unfolds, and the reader-narrator separation narrows to invisibility. Bessette's novel thus exposes a somber and deadly vision of the world more explicitly than in earlier works by his bold use of calculated spontaneity to pour forth a story of passion and death, and of the narrator's guilt-filled conscience at perhaps not having prevented that death. The world of *L'Incubation* is one of pettiness and anguish, remorse and despair; the absurdity of love is no less a truism than is the necessity of death, and, indeed, death, or the desire for some form of living death, presides over all other human actions which appear, by contrast, ludicrous or gratuitous.

Antinéa's suicide sets in motion the narrator's memory and the book's agonizing scrutiny of reasons and responsibility for past actions that led to the woman's death. All the major characters feel an overriding sense of guilt: Antinéa and Gordon for the adulterous relationship that might have led to the death of Antinéa's husband; Weingerter for having given sleeping pills to Antinéa to help alleviate her mental suffering but that she used to kill herself; Lagarde for not having acted to ward off the suicide. The monologue goes back in time, then forward in linear chronological fashion to the pivotal event, with the narrative consciousness cunningly leading the reader astray by insinuation as to the various characters' motivations and the situation's possible developments. Bessette molds his novel into a game of deception and deceit manipulated by a narrator obsessively preoccupied with a sense of measured (in)accuracy. Lagarde thus "plays" with the themes of guilt, the temptation to suicide, the impossibility of confrontation and communication as they affect the principal characters. He slyly sows clues to the novel's outcome throughout the book only to replace these by different decoys that entice the reader in other situational directions. Before the close each of the main characters will have been presented in the guise of victim—of his repressed phantasms, of circumstances beyond his control, of the lack of adequate communicability.

The "incubation" of the novel's title is the prolonged hatching period during which characters come to lose any fundamental certitude of their self-identity: a good example is Antinéa in her growing propensity toward self-annihilation. For the others, incubation takes the form of gradual disintegration of an intact sense of self under the weight of confusion and guilt in human relationships. Bessette gives his novel a surface structure wherein the narrator focuses attention on Gordon Blackwell and his dead-end situation (the reappearance of his former mistress in the presence of Gordon with wife and children), seemingly granting to Blackwell the status of protagonist; and a depth structure that reveals the true protagonist to be Antinéa in her lifelong dilemma rooted in childhood feelings of rejection and abandonment by her parents. In this and other respects, Bessette's technique recalls those of French "New Novelists" (Claude Simon and Alain Robbe-Grillet especially) who liberally use detective-story or suspense-novel techniques to dispense the psychology in their works. The book's narrator builds up Antinéa's "case" as he notes her increasing alienation from functioning reality, her bitterness and silent despair in coping with her lack of emotional stability, her stunted maturity and failure both in her marriage and in her love affair with Blackwell. Not having received the love and affection that she craved from the parents, Antinéa withdraws into herself out of feelings of shame and unworthiness, and thus is crippled in her ability to love others. She falls prey to an overwhelming anxiety neurosis which she is unable to handle because she fails to recognize its symptoms and search out its causes.

Far more complex in form and content than *Le Libraire*, *L'Incubation* reveals Bessette as a gifted craftsman of the novel genre. Under the influence of the "New Novel" in France he has written a work that plays a constant game with the unwary reader, as the character-narrator sets his multiple plot traps, advancing the story in various potential directions. The incubation refers thus not only to the novel's inner story, but to the outer narrative as well.

Les Anthropoïdes (The anthropoids), 1977, signals yet a new direction for Bessette, or rather an intensification of the formalistic aspect of his writing; more than in any other of his novels he pushes this propensity toward the purely verbal to a paroxysmal delirium. Pride of place is given to language as immense and infinite game; what is of utmost significance in *Les Anthropoïdes* is not the representational but the chimerical element of self-engendering text existing in an unending continuum or flux. Bessette does not concern himself with psychoanalytic verisimilitude here, nor with language as a verifiable component of fiction, but rather with the written word, with imagined and imaginary language that is autonomous and in no need of any recognizable outside referent that would justify it. Bessette moves away from the concept of language as referential narration and toward the fact of language as phantasm and metaphor. An innovative landmark in Quebec prose, *Les Anthropoïdes* stands as an exultant song of praise for the gift of speech, and of speech as the guarantor of memory and of understanding among men. The endless sentence of which the novel is composed (and which is exploded by numerous parenthetical deviations) transcribes a multiple narrative voice and telescopes interior monologues one into the other. A conventional third person, a reflexive third person, and a first person, comprise a kaleidoscope of optics for the reader to view the evolving world of the anthropoids.

Bessette subversively presents his novel as a quasi documentary, an imagined anthropology of evolution by way of tableaux concerning the life of the Kalahoumes and their struggles against ancestral souls, nature, and factious tribes. The various monologuists image the story of their race and, by their projections, elaborate an origin of the species, a sacred mythology of humanoid nature. As, in their mythical past, we move from the Kalahoumes to the Kalahoumides to the Gonkalokis, the humanoid resemblance is made more manifest in language, thought, and social, physical, and psychological structures. The entire novel might be considered an initiatory voyage back through time and space in search of a universal land which would assure a world of peace and compassion; the work, after all, has as its subtitle, a "novel of adventure(s)." The reader encounters the heroic endeavors of the Great Bao and, above all, the grand adventure of the written word incarnated by the narrator(s) under the composite name of Guito.

In stylized manner, Bessette's fantastic tale reveals a universe of religious and sexual practices, societal structures, and psychological obsessions, all imbued with a certain magical quality, an epic dimension that transcends any literal, representational reading of the work, and all sieved through Guito's stream-of-consciousness monologue. For that, Bessette invents an extraordinarily rich vocabulary made of neologisms and onomatopoeia, word deformations and transformations, a lexicon that is concrete rather than abstract, yet based in a perfectly intelligible syntax. Les Anthropoïdes is Bessette's audacious paean to human word and speech, one which contributes originality and innovation to Quebec literature.

His prose has thus evolved radically since the timely but relatively simplistic Le Libraire. While Le Semestre (The semester), 1979, contains essential Bessettian characteristics harking back to that early novel, it is infinitely more complex, thematically and technically. Bessette's stance in Le Semestre is that of the creative autobiographer who clasts icons and confabulates what Omer Marin, the work's past-future author and present character, calls a fantastic hybrid monster. The entire book might be placed under the rubric of half-fiction, half-autobiography. The transgression is flagrant and constant, but Bessette's rapacious, tongue-in-cheek irony rules out even that equation, at the same time that it underscores the explosive/ exploding nature of his writings.

The book adopts a spiral structure whereby the author/narrator/ character burrows ever deeper into the recesses of his psychic past, the meaning of present events during one university semester, and the traumatizing possibilities of oncoming old age and death. The triple componential elements determine the situations that propel movement forward: Marin's lengthy dissection of Gilbert La Rocque's *Serge d'entre les morts* (Serge from among the dead), his detailed analysis of obsessional dreams and phantasms, and a prolonged sexual encounter between the professor-protagonist and Sandra, one of his students. Marin/Bessette (novelists, critics, pedagogues both) and the reader are thus dealing with three novelistic strata continually sliding into one another or superimposed one upon the other: La Rocque's novel (the deepest level of psychic revelation for Marin and the novel's most profound architectural underpinning); Marin's multilayered monologues, which he envisions as a "future quasi novel which will probably be titled *Le Semestre*"; and Bessette's published novel (the outermost level and most convoluted).

Bessettian hermeneutics impose elaborate coding and decoding programs. Marin the pedagogue proffers an acerbic indictment of the contemporary higher education system in North America, while Marin as novelist alternately revels in and refuses psychocriticism, praises and damns Freud (the "Viennese Magus"), and Marin as critic voraciously discourses on modern Quebec literature. Marin . . . ? or Bessette . . . ? or Bessette posing as Marin . . . ? (Marin teaches at Princess University, Ontario; Bessette at Queen's University, Ontario.) *Le Semestre* might appear (falsely) to be a roman à clef in which Marin/Bessette indulges in abrasively humorous sallies against certain Quebec authors: for example, Jack MacFerron [Jacques Ferron], Âne Chambredebois [Anne Hébert's *Les Chambres de bois*], Butor-Ali Nonlieu [Victor-Lévy Beaulieu], and the unfortunate feminist Vinicole Brosseuse [Nicole Brossard]. The review *Servitude* [*Liberté*] is not spared, nor in Marin/Bessette's psychopolitics is the oedipolitical Fart, P.E.T. (French *pet* = fart) [Pierre Elliott Trudeau]. Bessette, furthermore, deforms titles of his own works as ironic distancing codes which he inserts liberally into *Le Semestre*.

Distance and intimacy, life and death, understanding and confusion, these constitute, throughout, the novel's basic pulsation. In a psychoanalytic reading it is not insignificant to note that at the outset Marin begins his quest for the primal scene (in the Freudian sense) and in the closing sequence of the book emits a prolonged primal scream (in the Janovian sense). And in a critico-scriptic reading it is no less significant that Marin refers on the second page to his virtually completed novel, and that the work's final words substantiate the reality and necessity of that novel, projected and written, that the reader has just concluded. For Bessette, the magus offers liberation, but the muse assures survival.

Jacques Godbout (1933–)

Jacques Godbout's novels appear to be moments of meditation upon forms of political commitment and means of achieving nationalistic self-identity. It should, however, be stressed that they are meditations, not actions; rather than flow into the actual, his protagonists' evolution stops within the realm of the virtual. The strong dose of optimism in his works is thus tempered by characters' seeming inability to break down certain barriers innate to their sociopolitical, cultural context. Godbout's ironic humor underscores this aspect of his characters' psychological makeup beginning with his first three novels, which he terms a trilogy, and continuing in the last two as the start of a new cycle in his novelistic output.

The significance and aim of the act of writing also lie at the center of Godbout's novels, in which the author posits writing as a force of the will and a source of freedom. It is solidly rooted in reality in order to better confront and question certain givens of modern social structures. Godbout thus conceives reality and writing as modes of both opposition and rapprochement, with satire the principal link between writing as tool and reality as matter. As in the case of Anne Hébert, Godbout assigns to the written word a strong magical power with which he builds his prose constructs and gives to each of them a liberating thrust outward from some constricting time/space. Each novel, save *Les Têtes à Papineau*, if not a realization of a new self in a transformed society, stands decidedly as a heightening of the protagonist's awareness of his identity within a "French Canadian" society that is in the process of becoming a "Quebec" society. Godbout's novels are peopled with divided, alienated figures, wanderers in search of themselves, and basically or ultimately concerned with the destiny of their native land. Whether the land be rejected or accepted or reconquered, the fact and future of Quebec remains the pivotal point for thematics that have already been seen in Quebec literature: dispossession and repossession. In this sense his novels are self-reflexive in that their protagonists learn to observe their actions and reactions as individuals within a larger collective sociopolitical unit that, once understood, must be changed.

L'Aquarium (The aquarium) appears in 1962, while the "Quiet Revolution" is in full swing, and its setting, a tropical country where blacks have undertaken a revolution to free their society, is not without patent links to the nationalist ideological preoccupations in Quebec at the time. The work's principal character, who remains nameless throughout, is a "French Canadian" (as opposed to "Quebec") artist, a loner-outcast entertaining no relationships between himself as an individual and the class to which he belongs. He consciously refuses any sense of identification and acknowledges the futility and meaninglessness of his existence in the closed moral world of the Casa Occidentale, where he and other "snails" wait out the revolution taking place around them. The character referred to as "He," whom the "snails" had allowed to be engulfed in quicksand, and his surrogate, Andrée ("He"'s former mistress), appear as false savior-figures that bring to the protagonist only the possibility of a personal, egotistical escape instead of a real redemption associated with the notion of collective hope. The antihero's future seems as empty as his present exile is devoid of substance.

The Casa Occidentale serves as a metaphor of society in general, with its inhabitants the object of the protagonist's observation. Through that protagonist Godbout indicts values inherent in love and death, religion and human communication, as he considers them to exist and function in contemporary society, that is, largely a matter of lack of courage and general indifference. As the novel progresses, the reader witnesses the growing moral disintegration of its characters and their passive concession to defeat; even the protagonist's final "liberation" from the Casa is a flight away from a feeling of powerlessness rather than a commitment to any constructive act of transformation. *L'Aquarium* stands as an intellectual rumination on the possibility of a revolution or the fact of a revolt that remains external to the individual, who is unable or unwilling to view it as a historical event in which he is directly involved. Boredom and cruelty, cowardliness and moral irresponsibility, reign supreme, a theme most recurrently expressed by the image of unending rain and humidity, locking the Casa's "snails" deeper into their fatuousness and turpitude.

The central character is not without lucidity in at least questioning the problems of isolation and commitment, ethics and history, but his self-probings merely reveal the extent of his erratic wanderings, his incapacity to establish moral and social rapports with the collective community, either the colonizers or the colonized. By the image of the Casa as a microcosm of the colonized country on the verge of decolonization, Godbout shows the danger posed to autonomy by individuals who, like his protagonist, possess a critical consciousness, an awareness of the ills of society, and yet fail to believe in any absolute value system or even a relative set of values that would justify human existence and the need for liberty, justice, and dignity among men. Godbout thus constructs his first novel on the universal thematics of decolonization within a larger framework of existential preoccupations, but which are tied to ethical, political, and nationalist movements in Quebec society in the late fifties or early sixties.

In *Le Couteau sur la table (Knife on the Table)*, 1965, Godbout shifts geography to Canadian territory, thereby giving to the novel as a whole a sense of spatial immediacy that the first novel lacked, and personalizes thematics which in *L'Aquarium* were more academic and intellectualized. The novel's central metaphor of the anglophone/francophone couple brings literally closer to home the fundamental dilemma of Quebec's linguistic and sociocultural duality, which in the sixties surfaced as the province's foremost object of political discussion. And it is to be recalled that Godbout's first three novels were written and published in the early to mid-sixties; the progression of the inherent themes in those works closely parallels the dimensions of developments in Quebec society during the same period.

Significantly, Godbout's principal character is again nameless and has not yet achieved the status of Quebecer; he remains the "errant French Canadian" torn between anglophone domination over a humbled people on the one hand, and an emerging francophone power and self-assertion on the other. The rhythm modulates from episodes of Anglo/Franco coexistence to scenes of francophone repudiation of oppression (a repudiation which, however, is a matter of word, not act) to repeated sequences of flight away from events and situations that beg to be faced squarely and honestly. *Le Couteau sur la table*'s protagonist stops short of active espousal of Quebec's independence movement, a flaw which Godbout stresses at his novel's close. While there is an urgent reference to terrorist acts in the cause of liberation, the antihero's knife remains on the table: Patricia, his anglophone mistress and image of the British conqueror, may be rejected in mind but not killed in fact. This double-edged renunciation is compounded by the strongly symbolic death of the protagonist's francophone mistress, Madeleine, and of the child she was to bear. Here, as in *L'Aquarium,* the principal character's personal past, marked by submission and humiliation, echoes the province's history of resignation and defeat. Neither is yet prepared to transcend tepid verbal revolt and actually engage in political revolution.

The novel's geographical cadre, perhaps above all else, records the dialectical tension between the themes of alienation from and identification with francophone ethnicity. After escapist flights to the United States and Mexico, the protagonist leaves Canada's anglophone western plains only to rediscover the basic linguistic, economic, cultural rupture within Montreal itself and the politically explosive rift separating its two major ethnic communities. The very geographic reality is enough to provoke an adumbration of awareness in the narrator-protagonist who is, however, more curious about his "discovery" than he is moved to act in consequence of it. The old safety of exile proves stronger than the risk of new ties to his native land. It must be pointed out, nonetheless, that Godbout dedicated his novel to the editorial team of the journal *Liberté* which lauded the virtues of the "Quiet Revolution," and that he himself, in his brief introduction, considers the novel a literary approximation of a cultural repossession. The reader is thus, from the outset, placed in a perspective that is geared, positively, toward the notions of decolonization and reappropriation of francophone autonomy on the North American continent. Unlike the narrator of *L'Aquarium,* who sides with neither colonizers nor colonized but chooses instead a self-centered destiny, the narrator of *Le Couteau sur la table* belongs to the colonized class and senses the necessary connection yet to be made between the individual and the collective community in any effort toward freedom from Anglo-Canadian and American domination.

Godbout's petit-bourgeois intellectual continues to incarnate the passive resignation of the "French-Canadian" whose anguish-ridden inquiry into his present resembles an exercise in self-mockery. The author underscores the nostalgic, stagnating aspect of his protagonist and his people in order to move them out of the quagmire of failure into the arena of future success. His later novels pursue that direction even further.

The eponymous hero of *Salut Galarneau!* *(Hail Galarneau!)*, 1967, acquires a name (François Galarneau) and in so doing assumes a measure of Quebecitude that neither of Godbout's previous protagonists had been able to attain. The recourse to exotic locale in *L'Aquarium* and to anglophone North America in *Le Couteau sur la table* disappear in favor of a strictly Quebec geography; and Jacques, François's brother who spends the requisite period of time in France, is quickly dispensed with in the book while François remains in the foreground throughout. Galarneau's difficult birth into and exultant acceptance of his francophone ethnicity inform the entire novel, just as his diary within the novel composes a lengthy meditation on the role of the individual in society and on the need for active association with the collective political community. Godbout's principal character here conjugates past, present, and future, realized through the primordial act of writing as the most efficacious tool for both personal and communal consciousness. It is by that very act that Galarneau acknowledges that writing must not become yet another means of evading, if not completely avoiding, reality; hence, after having walled himself into a cocoonlike existence deep within his diary notations, he draws upon his lucid assessment of his existential destiny, breaks down the walls he has erected, and reestablishes contact with his fellowmen.

Galarneau-Godbout uses satire and parody, irony and whimsical imagination in mediatory writing in order to understand reality more fully and thereby accept it if it is decently tolerable, or change it if circumstances so dictate. The novel's close is, however, as in the author's previous works, ambivalent, perhaps contradictory: Galarneau recognizes the salubriousness of the simultaneity (not antagonism) between reality and writing, and his sense of the collective entity bodes well toward unashamed acceptance of his ethnicity. His departure for the United States—very much a prime alien and alienating force in Godbout's novelistic universe—bodes far less well for the notion of Quebecers' determination to assert their ethnicity.

As will be the case in *D'Amour, P.Q.*, it is a female figure who is largely responsible for Galarneau's initial commitment to writing, first for the pleasure of storytelling, ultimately to scrutinize objectively the reality that surrounds him and to condemn the lot of colonized Quebecers, although his reticence will prevent him from providing a cogent contribution toward solving the historical dilemma facing contemporary Quebec. By contrast with the earlier novels, *Salut Galarneau!* sets forth, at best, the concept of a certain reconciliation with self and community. Its protagonist himself, though he comes from a bourgeois intellectual family, belongs to the working class by choice, unlike the antiheroes of the first two novels who, furthermore, were entrapped between two intensely opposed ideological poles to an extent that Galarneau never experiences. His observation post is firmly ensconced in the proletarian colonized camp; his attitude is downright aggressive by comparison with that of his predecessors who also lacked the comparatively lucid distance he brings to his appraisal of the social and political climate of Quebec and Canada.

Galarneau's worldview is relativistic, for he understands that exploited classes themselves exploit—Quebec itself is not spared, nor is the American enemy whose economical, cultural, and political domination must at all costs be counterattacked. This "attack" for the protagonist is essentially by means of literature, which mode he perceives as not only socially useful but personally necessary for a rebirth from a condition of mental inactivity to an avowal of political activism, a repossession of self and history. Godbout presents his novel, this entire birth process, as an expanded metaphor of Quebec's arousal in the 1960s from a years-long quietism toward a possible, if not ultimate liberation. *Salut Galarneau!* comprises a literary documentation, one might say manifesto, of that nationalist movement.

The writer figure, who had already hovered about in Godbout novels, occupies the center and forefront in *D'Amour, P.Q.* (Thomas D'Amour, P.Q.), 1972, in which Thomas d'Amour is himself a novelist in the process of penning a novel very much in the conventional classic French mold. Mariette and Mireille, d'Amour's secretaries, are the two intervening forces who dismantle his estranged versions of the "French novel," rebuilding them in the cast of the autochthonous "Quebec novel." Godbout thus grafts the social and political implications of *D'Amour, P.Q.* onto the narrative of a native Quebec writer's coming to terms with his own authentic cultural and linguistic reality. In *Le Couteau sur la table* Madeleine, the woman-as-country character, did not live because the time was not yet ripe for Quebec's reappropriation of its selfhood; Marise, in *Salut Galarneau!*, was at least able to instigate Galarneau to write and through writing to accept his Quebecitude. In *D'Amour, P.Q.* the two female characters assume, from the outset, their full Quebec identity and act as catalysts for D'Amour to recognize the necessity, right, and duty to seize the natural reality around him as legitimate material for the imagination, for the transformation of reality. Godbout's novel elaborates the rites of passage from enslavement and shame to freedom and pride.

Through the mythical figure of woman-as-country Godbout enables his protagonist to superimpose the materiality of writing upon the historicity of his people; art and life form one inseparable but clearly defined entity. Mariette/Mireille claim and proclaim their geographic roots, their cultural origins, their present domination over Quebec time/space, and, implicitly, their future social and political autonomy. This is their legacy to Thomas d'Amour: no painful doubts and refusals, no escape or exile, no humble questionings, but personal and collective affirmation of one's existence and a legitimately adequate adaptation of literature to that ethnic existence. D'Amour gradually sheds the personality of an intellectual elite writer removed from his native environment and slavishly dependent upon a foreign culture; by accepting himself he can accept his own society and in the process equate, in writing and act, the singular and the universal.

Just as Godbout's preceding novels were written in the context of the "Quiet Revolution," so *D'Amour, P.Q.* was published shortly after the "Parti Québécois" (P.Q.) became a formal party to be reckoned with in Quebec politics. Godbout clearly inserts this political field into his narrative, given, not insignificantly, to the instigator-character Mireille more than to D'Amour or the narrator. Indeed, Mireille shifts from character to coauthor of D'Amour's new novel, and together they form a "love cell" of the "Front de Libération du Kébec" (read "Québec"; the revolutionary group of the time), emitting press communiqués reflecting the ideological countercurrents of the early 1970s in Quebec. The new nationalism focus is the very essence of *D'Amour, P.Q.* which, parodistically, contains and denies the societal visions of earlier Godbout works. The setting of D'Amour's first novel cannot but recall *L'Aquarium;* his second attempt mimics the American adventure tale, thus evoking the

United States escape routes in *Le Couteau sur la table* and, to a lesser extent, *Salut Galarneau!* Mireille instinctively rejects both and counsels D'Amour to return and acknowledge his own people and their history at a time of critical social and political change. "P.Q." is both Godbout's approving nod in the direction of Quebec autonomy as well as an ironic reference to and refusal of the status of mere province (Province of Quebec). Taken together, the communiqués, in fact, go beyond the nationalist concept to form a global notion of an international community in which all societies are equal and integral partners. The author thus deftly telescopes into *D'Amour, P.Q.* all his previous novelistic incarnations and then transcends these to embrace a new fraternal order based on self-acceptance and an authentic value system that is at once socially necessary and historically valid.

Godbout structures *L'Isle au dragon (Dragon Island)*, 1976, on a mythological foundation composed of treasures and dragons, princesses and sacrificial offerings. Geography once again plays a crucial role, the "Isle Verte" (Green Island) here being the symbolic equivalent of the "island" of Quebec and the targeted victim of appropriation by a multinational American-based company headed by a certain William T. Shaheen Jr. The novel pits its narrator-writer, Michel Beauparlant, against Shaheen, as Beauparlant attempts to maintain intact both a land and a society in the face of its inhabitants' possible acceptance of a foreign takeover and the resultant dispossession of the island's people for a promised greener pasture elsewhere, thanks to the ever-present power of moneyed rulers. Geographic space thus has not only structural importance in the book's narrative but also political overtones in the work's thematic underpinnings. At stake is the positive social effort to protect an autonomous homeland from the nefarious influence of outside forces that wish only to exploit the homeland for their own self-serving motives. Shaheen's project is to choose an especially beautiful and unspoiled setting as his company's future atomic dump-site. Beauparlant's counterbalancing project, which aims at preserving the sociomoral integrity of the "island," dovetails with Godbout's recurring theme of outright liberation.

Like previous novels, *L'Isle au dragon* possesses an open-ended quality that stresses Quebec's eventual and ultimately necessary political awakening. The temporal cadres likewise resemble those of the earlier works insofar as the narrator harks back to the past to recount the antagonistic relationship that develops between him and Shaheen, and writes his diary in the present to relate his individual and collective reactions to the unfolding situation. The confluence of past and present then enables the narrator (and the book's ending) to focus upon a future possibility of national autonomy. *L'Isle au dragon* presents the vision of a utopia that would prevail over the decrepitude of capitalistic societies; in this respect, the work recalls the unanimist worldview that Godbout offered in *D'Amour, P.Q.*

Michel Beauparlant, as his surname indicates, "speaks well" but also realizes that his campaign against invasion and erosion by the capitalist machine may not succeed. Yet—and this is a constant in Godbout's works—the ironic, satirical distance that the author imprints upon his novels gives the reader the impression that the worthiest of human endeavors is the battle to gain the upper hand over a certain fatalism, over seemingly unstoppable historical developments. Hence the choice of the forename Michel, recalling Saint Michael and the dragon. Beauparlant's entire life-attitude tends toward his (and the reader's) belief in affirmation of self-identity, reappropriation of native land, and future sociopolitical association that would effectively replace past and present separation (in the sense of alienation) by separatism.

L'Isle au dragon is in the tradition of the novel of quest (with its ancillary allegorical resonances) within which Godbout places his collective "islander" protagonist, a familiar colonized figure, victimized here not by anglophone Canada but by worldwide corporate imperialism. Shaheen's Pennsylvania and Texas International has tentacles reaching far beyond the economic sphere; Godbout presents it, thinly disguised, as the all-too-familiar American capitalist power subversively imposing its political and ideological exploitation on a global scale. The fate of Green Island symbolizes the extent to which that subversion has penetrated and reshaped the very heart of Canadian and, specifically, Quebec society. Godbout's novel, open to multiple interpretations, closes in typically ambivalent fashion. Beauparlant is alone in resisting the cultural invader, receiving support neither from the community ready to sell out, nor from the government, itself manipulated by the American aggressor; and yet, in this fantasy fable, Michael wins out against the dragon and wins the princess as his reward.

In *Les Têtes à Papineau* (Papineau, the bicephalous monster), 1981, Godbout continues to play one of his favorite games: mixing and mismatching reality and fiction. The author's statement on the book jacket deliberately misleads the reader into assuming that Charles-François Papineau, "bicephalous monster," actually existed in the same phenomenal manner as the Dionne quintuplets and was born in Montreal in 1955. For Godbout there is as much, or as little, verisimilitude in invention as there is in fact, and the two constantly intermesh in life as in art. *Les Têtes à Papineau* perhaps most closely resembles *Salut Galarneau!*, not only in this formal aspect of writing as game but also in its thematic ramifications. And like *Le Couteau sur la table* and *D'Amour, P.Q.*, it is solidly anchored in a topical political context, in this case the victory of the "Parti Québécois" at the polls followed by the defeat of the party's referendum on sovereignty-association with the rest of Canada. Once again, and more threatening than ever in recent times, the double-headed monster rears up. Quebecers must face the fact and the consequences of their dual identity as both francophone Canadians and Quebecers, their double immersion in anglophone and francophone communities. *Les Têtes à Papineau* is, in this light, a novel of choice: the political and cultural, social and economic choices that the province must make in shaping its future.

The referendum results, based on Quebecers' own vote on the question, would indicate a capitulation to maintaining their colonized, minority status within anglophone Canada, to remaining what they have been for so long: French-Canadians. Godbout's novel presents a far more drastic vision of Quebec's future, however. While still bicephalous, Charles-François claims to be in ideologically opposing camps, a situation which, symbolically, appears to rule out the feasibility of sovereignty-association. Following a brain operation that fuses both heads into a unicephalous being, Charles F. Papineau is transformed into a unilingual being as well: an anglophone. The last-chapter thematics, which have always been of first importance in Godbout's novels, here assume larger than ever significance. The last chapter consists, in effect, of a letter from Charles F. to the francophone publishing firm with which Charles-François had signed a contract for publication of their diary. It now becomes impossible for Charles F. to write the last chapter of that diary in French. The radical implications of Godbout's allegory seem clear enough: the possible last chapter of Charles-François's diary is the metaphorical equivalent of the potential last chapter in Quebec's history. Just as the diary's finale (if it is to exist at all, however, since Charles F.

merely states that he will study the matter) is destined to be written in English, so does Quebec's ultimate fate seem doomed to amalgamation with anglophone Canada and submission to the United States technological and cultural superpower.

Coming after a series of novels that progressed in a forward, positive direction in their treatment of the Quebec theme, *Les Têtes à Papineau* offers an unexpectedly grim reassessment of that theme.

Jacques Ferron (1921–1985)

Different bibliographies list Jacques Ferron's prose fiction works as, variously, "tales," (or "long tales"), or "narratives," or "novels." Some claim *Le Ciel de Québec (The Penniless Redeemer)*, 1969, and, perhaps, *Le Salut de l'Irlande* (Ireland's salvation), 1970, to be the only "true novels" that Ferron has authored. Be that as it may, the works (which for the sake of concision and simplification will here be referred to as novels) bear intimate interrelationships thematically and technically and will therefore be examined by way of a composite overview. Similar to Jacques Godbout in a number of respects, Ferron roots his fiction solidly in contemporary Quebec reality and, never losing sight of that reality, fabricates fanciful mythologies and a history often built on legendry and phantasmagoria. Characters' efforts at redemption tilt, in final analysis, toward future possession of self and country; the traditional past yields to a renewing present, despair to hope, quiescence to assertive action. Ferron's protagonists are or become fiercely combative against death, which, in the author's fictional world, is equated with the inexistence of Quebec as an autonomous political and social identity. For Godbout, Ferron, and Hubert Aquin, perhaps more than any other recent Quebec novelists, Quebec consistently and insistently comprises the raw material for their writings and has pride of place in them.

That is not tantamount to saying that Ferron is thereby a rabid believer in the province's nationalist independence, as some critics are led to believe by such works as *La Nuit* (Night), 1965, and its revised version, *Les Confitures de coings (Quince Jam)*, 1972. Both are reworkings of the Faust legend (a legend which reappears in *Le Saint-Elias* [*The Saint-Elias*], 1972, in the character of Dr. Fauteux). François Ménard sells his soul to his anglophone double Frank Archibald Campbell, and in so doing renounces his social, cultural, and linguistic identity. In each version François's initiatory nocturnal voyage carries him from a sort of purgatory existence (symbolized by Montreal's Longueil suburb) into Hell (symbolized by the city and the morgue where he meets Frank), as he is chauffeured there across the Saint Lawrence River (the River Styx) by Alfredo Carone (Charon, the ferryman for dead souls). During the course of this quest for authentic self, François sheds his persona after killing Frank with poisoned quince jam, and at night's close he wends his way back home to his wife Marguerite, now resurrected as a being in her own right and not a mere passive appurtenance in François's hypocritical life. One notable change, however, in the 1972 version reveals the author's doubts about, if not his refusal of the independentist movement as opposed to a better balanced notion of sovereignty-association. The "Effelquois" (member of the radical and, in 1970, terrorist FLQ, Front de Libération du Québec), whom François notices removing English-language signs on street posts, disappears entirely. In *Le Ciel de Québec* (and *Le Saint-Elias*) especially, Ferron likewise enlarges the scope of his vision toward more universal statements of the human condition.

Le Ciel de Québec offers a multilayered portrait of society in Quebec and environs during 1937 and 1938, centering around a nucleus of clergymen, writers, and politicians, and their diverse associates, including a vividly realized Irish coachman, several unforgettable native Americans, another and somewhat different Dr. Cotnoir from that in the 1962 *Cotnoir (Dr. Cotnoir)*, and a whole gamut of others ranging from painters, journalists, and generals to prostitutes and pimps. The work exuberantly amalgamates the real and the imaginary, juxtaposed, interpenetrating, each shaping, enriching, and deforming the other. Real people appear as themselves in their authentic social, literary, or historical setting, then rub elbows with outrageous caricatures of other real-life personages, or become enmeshed in purely fictional passages of surrealistic slapstick and satire. The Orpheus legend is retold, with Saint-Denys Garneau, one of Quebec's leading poets, cast in the unflattering role of Orpheus, and his cousin, novelist-poet Anne Hébert, faring no better in her cameo part. As so often in Ferron's writings, there is a savior-figure, in this case the child "Rédempteur Fauché" ("the penniless Redeemer"), the name borrowed from a news item relating the fate of an individual found murdered in the 1960s after having been implicated as an underling in a series of criminal arsons. The author wryly calls Rédempteur's mother Marie, and her husband, a carpenter, Joseph. Though the novel's principal events occur during a comparatively short time in the late 1930s, Ferron does not hesitate to elaborate that fictional present by recounting Quebec and Canadian history back to the nineteenth century and earlier, and projecting into a future among the dead which could not have taken place before the 1960s.

Ferron's formidable talents are perhaps at peak strength in *Le Ciel de Québec*. He repeatedly demonstrates his ability to give the reader quickly a complete sense of a character, resulting, however, in the concomitant disadvantage that only rarely does one feel a character's development through time. The masterly use of the telling detail, the keen ear for dialogue, the sense of compassion, and, in particular, the comic verve constitute eminent traits of his writing techniques. Ferron is also not averse to borrowing proven comic devices from other authors. For example, Monsignor Camille (based on Monseigneur Camille Roy, rector of Laval University), one of his more endearing personages, engages in conversations with the Lord which are patently modeled on those of Don Camillo in Giovanni Guareschi's *The Little World of Don Camillo*.

As in the author's other works, plot assumes relative unimportance, and the reader's interest focuses on the personality portraits and on a succession of mainly self-contained anecdotes. Ferron's narrative methods persistently subvert any story line that might have structured significant novelistic-style plots, most commonly by leaving them less fascinating than the piquant, incongruous smaller incidents which surround them. For example, the event that serves as the novel's framework, the decision to establish a new parish in the village of the Chiquettes, separating it from the parish governed by the larger village of Saint-Magloire, leads, by the close of the novel, to the building of a new church for the new parish. But there is never any question as to whether this goal will be accomplished, never any suspense, merely minor obstacles to be overcome, and, most significantly, no character among those to whom the author directs our attention ever seems particularly concerned about the eventual results of the project. That is, founding the parish of Sainte-Eulalie changes in no wise the lives of *Le Ciel de Québec*'s principal characters.

On another level, one can interpret the work as a novel of initiation, the tale of the coming of age of Frank-Anacharsis Scot, who narrates the conclusion. But in final analysis the crisis of his maturation takes place when he decides to abandon his missionary duties among the Inuits, that is, before he is introduced as a character in the second quarter of the narrative. The reader witnesses his first visit to a bordello, his departure from his parents' home, and his experiments aimed at total identification with Quebec's francophone population—episodes rich in comic inventiveness, but none representing more than the elucidation of a few final details in a process that had already been largely terminated.

Ferron's penchant for comedy reflects but one aspect of a global attitude that is enthusiastically life-embracing; the interstices between the myriad humorous passages often underscore the weightiest of preoccupations, including serious discussion of literature and art, some astute political analysis, tangents of theology and philosophy, and a panoply of the history of the period that lends the book an aura of chronicle as well as fiction. Similarly, social criticism plays a predominant part, eloquently illustrated by Ferron's presentation of the Chiquettes, a fictitious Indian tribe. Exploited by unscrupulous politicians, despised and denigrated by everyone, they symbolize to their Saint-Magloire neighbors a repository of crime and ignorance. In reality, as the cardinal recognizes, the denizens of Saint-Magloire depend on the Chiquettes in order to maintain their own feelings of superiority and smug self-righteousness. (One among many elements linking Ferron's writing with mythological archetypes is that the savior-figure is born into this downtrodden group.) The dialectics between these two unequal villages provides a topos that occurs in multiple imagistic forms throughout the novel, as, time and again, the "superior" of the two can derive not merely its definition but its very being from the "inferior."

It soon becomes apparent that a parallel situation divides the city of Quebec, with its bourgeois "Haute Ville" and its working class "Basse Ville." And even a superficial reading of the image imposes recognition of its political implications on a national scale, the province of Quebec performing the same function for Canada that the village of the Chiquettes does for Saint-Magloire. In a display of passionate rhetoric during the visit of three prelates to the Chiquettes (the visit of the three kings to the young "Rédempteur"), an old Indian woman, who would die that very night, stresses that the Chiquettes' territory, small though it be, gives access to the entire sky. Her words are echoed at book's end in those of the carpenter Joseph, striving to build the church of the newly separated

parish, who points out that their sky is as large as Quebec's—and
that all the children of God must be ready unashamedly to take
that which rightfully belongs to them.

Ferron's thoughts run parallel to those that Godbout expresses in
L'Isle au dragon: he castigates the concept of progress as of necessity
beneficial and posits the notion that modern capitalist society blinds
man to any higher good and, by a process of reification, empties
him of human compassion and understanding. Both novelists appeal
to new humanizing forces that would unite rather than separate the
political and the cultural and bind spiritual needs to social claims.
La Charrette (The Cart), 1968, and *Le Salut de l'Irlande* highlight
this basic tenet in Ferron's entire canon: an ethical concern that
envisions economics and aesthetics, art and labor, inner imagination
and outer reality, as overlapping spheres of activity that cannot but
be taken as a whole if society is to be purged of Church-imposed
guilt and freed of government-sanctioned defilement and bondage.
Hence in Ferron's works appears the conceptual value of variant
images of light and dawn as heralds of renascence, of a fundamentally
renewed if not totally new world that opposes debasement and
injustice in favor of plenitude in salvation. *Le Salut de l'Irlande* is
nothing if not, embryonically, the salvation of humanity itself. By
contrast, the image of night represents the darker powers of domination and alienation, cynicism and pessimism (Godbout's novels
are, in truth, more heavily weighted by this negative energy), the
dispossession-death of self and homeland. The image takes on its
most obvious and elaborate configurations in *La Nuit/Les Confitures
de coings* but returns, for instance, in the hellish regions adumbrated
in *La Charrette* in which the boatman of Hades is also prominent
once again. For Ferron, this dialectics of individual human life and
death, of collective sociopolitical servitude and freedom, invariably
leads to the triumph of future national brotherhood, but no less to
the promise of universal fraternity. It is precisely this aspect that
lends a cosmic dimension to virtually all of Ferron's writings.

The fantastic and epic, chronicle and parable, intermix in his
fictional constructs, but it is only mischievously that he presents
the world as apparently mere spectacle. The stance recalls Godbout
once again (e.g., *Salut Galarneau!* or *D'Amour, P.Q.*): ethics and
aesthetics, fact and fancy, can be disengaged one from the other
only at the sure risk of disembodying each of them from any meaningful context and isolating them into senseless entities. Ferron as

author proposes what Galarneau as character discovers, namely, that imaginative creation (in this case fiction, but by extension any creative art form) is neither escapism nor withdrawal; on the contrary, its bases are firmly set in a surrounding tangible reality, and it provides the required means and courage to anchor even more solidly in the complexities of that reality. The eponymous hero in *Cotnoir*, Father Tourigny and Dr. Fauteux in *Le Saint-Elias*, Connie Haffigan in *Le Salut de l'Irlande*, Tinamer de Portanqueu in *L'Amélanchier (The Juneberry Tree)*, 1970, all attest to this quintessential Ferronian principle. To use the latter protagonist's lexicon, the "good side of things" will eventually win out over "the bad side of things" provided one aggressively (and permanently) fights against doubt and defeatism.

Ferron's spectacular texts, his parabolic books, are thus modes of approach to identifiable sociopolitical situations in contemporary Quebec, as they are echoes of infinitely vaster moral conundrums. *La Nuit/Les Confitures de coings* and *La Charrette* by their oneiric, infernal quality and their geographic imagery reflect not only the specifically Quebec dilemma of life in what Ferron calls "an uncertain land," but also larger-than-Quebec questions of desacralization of goodness and innocence, justice and commitment, under the oppressive imperialist masters of evil. These are incarnated most obviously by the presences of Bélial and Rouillé, guardian of Hades, in *Les Confitures de coings*, by Carone in *La Nuit*, and somewhat more elusively by the recurring character of Frank Archibald Campbell. Carone's taxi as the ferry of dead souls and deadened humans reappears as the cart that gives its name to *La Charrette*. In all three novels the highly charged images of the bridge spanning the Saint Lawrence/Styx, and of the city as luminous, enchanted castle snaring the unwary underscore the multiple levels of the work's representational significance.

Geographical symbolism in Ferron's fiction is often of a dual nature, at once specifically Quebec, but also technocratic capitalist societies in general. Though clearly not a regionalist author in the traditional acceptation of the term, Ferron chooses the city and the suburbs as imagistic figurations of possession and dispossession, belonging and alienation, of creation and stultification in contemporary man. In *La Nuit/Les Confitures de coings* and *La Charrette* the city circumscribes both the negative and positive poles: it is a site of death but also of rebirth. The suburbs, similarly, evoke a sense of isolation, loss, and void in relation to the city, but they compose the only extant links to the countryside, that is, to nature that permits the denunciation of imposture and offers freedom from the yoke of imperialist systems. In *Le Saint-Elias* the city of Trois-Rivières and the village of Batiscan assume roughly the same dipole values (articulated by Monsignor Laflèche and Father Tourigny), as do the large village of Saint-Magloire and the tiny village of the Chiquettes in *Le Ciel de Québec*. Thus, in his own allegorical manner, Ferron, throughout his work, seeks to portray the invidious interplay between universal good and immemorial evil; his novels are imagined battlefields on which towering gods and dwarfed demons war to a not-altogether-conclusive end. Ferron writes parables about reality's inescapable paradoxes, focusing particularly on ideological conflicts and contradictions that take shape in fictions made of magic and the marvelous, reason and the illogical.

His production not only represents Quebec but constructs it and re-creates it in a global image-as-fact that sheds the distorting influences of Church morality, of anglophone Canadian linguistic interference, and of socioeconomic domination by the United States. Dr. Cotnoir's redemption of Emmanuel anecdotally signifies the salvation of Quebec, the "uncertain country," and its movement away from exile toward stable self-possession. Without denying the historical past, indeed, remembering and utilizing that past as a hedge against future Canadian and American reductionist policies, Ferronian protagonists set out, in their status as present social beings, to force Quebec into a condition that would be neither total separation (i.e., unrealistic independentism) nor invisible fusion (i.e., craven servility). From *Cotnoir* to *Le Saint-Elias* (and in his theater as well) Jacques Ferron peoples his works with savior-figures, characters who not only save their individuality from immersion into alien cultural mechanisms but also stand as guarantors of Quebec society's ultimate freedom and preservation.

Louise Maheux-Forcier (1929–)

Louise Maheux-Forcier's trilogy, *Amadou* (Fire), 1963, *L'Ile joyeuse* (The joyous island), 1964, *Une Forêt pour Zoé* (A forest for Zoé), 1969, comprises an initiatory voyage in which Nathalie, *Amadou*'s heroine, evokes the omnipresence of the young Anne with whom she had come to know her first love. In the nocturnal flashback that provides the structure for the book, the narrator filters her entire life through that sacral moment, exploded at the outset of the work in cosmic, mythical terms. Within *Amadou*'s novelistic world Anne may or may not have actually existed; she might be a necessary figment of Nathalie's imagination, the keystone to creating a personal mythology that would repel her restrictive moral and religious upbringing.

Maheux-Forcier unfolds her novel as a parable equating Anne with Nathalie's beloved maple tree, planted on the day of her birth. Both are conceived as phenomena transcending any specificity of time and space, as sources and incarnations of Truth and Beauty, as bearers of a morality of Love to counterbalance conventional social and spiritual norms. The text makes it clear, however, that the compensation that they offer for those norms may be no more than illusory; and it is precisely at the dawn of the protagonist's anguish-ridden night that she kills her husand, the representative of prevailing mores, and sets her house afire, destroying herself and the love letters from Sylvia, the surrogate Anne figure. The rebirth of love is not meant to be, for Sylvia has but usurped Anne in an effort to eradicate what must remain the unique, irrevocable moment of Nathalie's existence: a love-as-friendship that can be preserved intact and unsullied only in death.

Throughout *Amadou* the sensual experience is invoked in grand imagistic contexts: Nathalie mobilizes all her fairy-tale powers to create a terrestrial paradise of the good and the beautiful, of happiness and plenitude, which she then peoples with Anne the flawless. An oneiric will informs much of the novel as Nathalie speaks of seeing as in a dream, of prolonging a dream. Shaped into an invented princess, she is destined for an encounter with a perfect image of Love and Truth beyond the confines of this world. Although Nathalie remains open to new relationships, heterosexual and homosexual, inevitably the golden visage of Anne dictates a refusal of them as dishonest and invalid. Seemingly accepting her bisexuality, Nathalie nevertheless reverts to an ethos adumbrated by Anne and lived in the homosexual love that they shared. She is impelled to destroy her husband Julien, for he considers Nathalie's "fabled" liaison with Anne and her "real" one with Sylvia as blemishes to be extirpated.

Maheux-Forcier underscores the notion of an adolescent love that is very much a matter of serenity and joy, and not passion, a love that must be eternal, indifferent to sex, age, reason, and law, a love that is less sexuality than a sensuality haloed with purity and child-like innocence. Adult love appears rather as possession and sub-mission, as a caricature of that sense of the marvelous which instinct bears with it. The freedom Nathalie seeks contradicts the egotism and solitude that her father inculcated and that forbade all contact and friendship as opiate myth. What she yearns for, and what Anne brings to her, is a relationship that is at once a sharing of personalities and a preservation of the individual self. For Nathalie, Anne is both a friend and a lover in experiencing a sensuality often described in moral terms of tenderness and admiration, in aesthetic terms of beauty and perfection. Theirs is a union of souls that can be known only in the plenitude of the instant as an ephemeral but unforgettable work of art, a gratuitous chimera.

Nathalie admits that she is incapable of understanding the reality that surrounds her, but she is intensely adept at imagining what she calls fugitive visions. Indeed, the novel often gives the impres-sion of a fable cast under a spell; the narrator presents herself and her double, Anne, as creatures living out a child's dream of a cavern full of wonders in which Nathalie reigns as fay. She dwells in a Romanesque chapel in which she (re)creates enchanted atmospheres all revolving about the theme of chaste love and the resplendent but invisible presence of Anne. Nathalie refers to this Norman chapel as the heart of her story, that is, the essence of her being. It is in this sequence that the author develops some of the most highly charged and poetically beautiful images of *Amadou*. Dream and reality intertwine in an atemporal setting, the religiosity of which establishes Anne and Sylvia as rival goddesses vying for the narrator's fidelity. In this decor that begets astonishment and discovery, the theme and image of the luminous canticle reach their apogee. Throughout the novel Anne's radiantly blond hair had become for Nathalie a talisman made of precious metal. Nathalie now meta-morphoses a chapel's yellow hangings into walls of sunlight, trans-forms empty echoes into the mournful rhapsodic beauty that transcribes her painful and failed efforts at realizing the perfect fusion of soul and body. The image of Anne's flowing mane is immediately as-sociated with Nathalie's tree; it also applies to Sylvia, become a divinity accomplishing ritual gestures with a magical chalice. Near the book's close the images recur as Sylvia attempts to free Nathalie from the memory of the dead Anne.

In final analysis *Amadou's* poeticized sensuality is perhaps accounted for by its protagonist's repressive Catholic background; her mother's constant admonitions bring about deep-seated feelings of guilt. Upon learning of the death of Gaspard, the pet dog, Nathalie, not insignificantly, rushes forward to protest her innocence; Anne's death by drowning remains ambiguous and Nathalie's reaction to it exudes an uncertain sense of responsibility. It is only when she can believe the absence of feelings of culpability in Sylvia that Nathalie can accept her penchant for fabulation. Compensating for the pernicious influence of religion's notions of good and evil and desirous of justifying homosexual love, *Amadou's* heroine makes of sexuality a poetically moral sensuality, while fashioning herself and her life into poetry.

Like the protagonist in *Amadou,* Isabelle in *L'Ile joyeuse* is an adult looking back upon a pivotal experience in the ritualistic passage from childhood through adolescence to adulthood. At the ages of fifteen and sixteen Nathalie and Isabelle rebel against the yoke of social conventions and moral tenets imposed upon them by fanatically religious mother-figures whose piety, directly centered on obsessions of the flesh, takes on for both characters a clearly sexual connotation. In *Amadou* Nathalie attempts to counteract the religious enigma and the unhealthy curiosity it provokes by molding a Truth and an Aesthetics removed from the mundane world. For Isabelle, early adolescence proves to be the most tormented and erotic period of her life, for which she seeks a palliative by imagining a universe where she can evolve alone and free of all strictures. The elaboration, destruction, and ultimate restoration of this personal mythology structures *L'Ile joyeuse.*

Maheux-Forcier's heroine, like those of the two other works of the trilogy, must deal with and try to accept her homosexuality, a fact that is moralized in musical terms and poetic imagery; her love for Julie is a composition in a major chord, Julie herself a creature of mane all fire and flame. Sensuality and shared love are lived in a tonality that annihilates dissonance and brings with it an intimacy of friendship and communion in states of quietude. Images of light blend with the musical, as when Julie's words illuminate concrete reality, and by a sortilege compose the source of a renascence to life. Isabelle invents what she calls luminous reason that will change pitiable reality into the marvelous. As a being of moon and clouds she forges her world of legends, the quintessence of which dates to her childhood. If certain of these legends concocted by a credulous sixteen-year-old come to be demythified during Isabelle's heterosexual affair with Stéphane, a mature Isabelle's visionary powers will reimprint on her life the lost magic of childhood. Where earlier she escaped the banal routine of daily existence to step into her creations, she later sheds the immense weight of boredom by means of nomadic mirages and imaginary voyages.

The joyous island of the book's title is the central image around which Maheux-Forcier articulates the entire novel. A temple beyond even the reach of memory, beyond time and space, it is another planet spoken of in terms of a cosmic union of human and natural forces. The island is a portable and liberating myth that enables Isabelle to transform other realities in the quest for her true reason for existing. Stéphane's sexuality will thus be considered the false light of her childhood, while the sensual love experience with Julie represents its candid luminosity, the inexorable duty of self-recognition which in turn allows the strength to assume not only an inalienable freedom but also the absurdity of life and the certitude of death. For Maheux-Forcier, this notion of love and truth associated with Isabelle and Julie's physical relationship is diametrically opposed to the tyrannical and the possessive; it stresses, rather, that physical possession is little or nothing compared to a giving and receiving that refuses sacrifices and concessions. The author, imagist above all, presents the theme by way of a solemn processional with Isabelle the priestess holding high the ostensorium containing the sacred host, the secret of the ceremony: a peaceful yet intensely shared tenderness. As in *Amadou,* Maheux-Forcier here underlines the key concept that sensuality is a purificatory morality.

The golden island and its birches serve as means for Isabelle to poeticize her vision of the world, to protect herself from deception and suffering by creating a universe apart, for herself and in itself. Isabelle's and Julie's dark, paltry room becomes a sunflower of light-emitting petals; its shabby blue rug forms a river around the bed and a straw mat is Isabelle's sandy isle. The episode is significant, for it reveals both the fragility of such poetic reconstructions and Isabelle's tenacity to live within her fabulous geography. As glows of gold and blue irradiate the room, she becomes aware that her "poem" is merely a child's tale, punctured by memories of solitude, pain, and humiliation. Hence she weaves larger tapestries from childhood images; through invented words and phantasms Maheux-

Forcier's heroine realizes a happiness that aspires to immortality and eternity.

The adult figures, even Julie, come to incarnate the loss of the dream of childhood; they possess the desire to destroy in Isabelle what has been destroyed in themselves. Violence, cruelty, madness, submission comprise so many manifestations of this destructive force, of adult sexuality, against which the protagonist reacts by making herself a cartographer of fantastic countries of creative solitude, of fire and magic, and, above all, landscapes of childhood. Isabelle accepts the impossibility of total love and happiness, the evanescence of human communication, but she also accepts the signal importance of the play between guise and honesty in relations with others and her own responsibility in living out what might have been truth but was in fact lie.

In *L'Ile joyeuse*'s short final chapter Isabelle has, after a number of years, come upon Julie and Stéphane in a tawdry nightclub where Julie, once a budding concert pianist, now plays with a mediocre pickup band. Maheux-Forcier's expanded imagery transcribes Isabelle's shattered reality: she feels herself caught in an apocalyptic tempest somewhere between music and the end of the world; Julie's beauty has turned into ugliness. In the midst of this demonic setting a child suddenly bursts one of the club's balloons, likened to a moon, an action that triggers an upheaval in Isabelle and reawakens her quest for ideal beauty and truth, enabling her to shed years of accumulated void in a night of deliverance. Having lived lives other than her own and expected solutions to absurdity and uselessness from the outside, she now is capable of reaching within herself to revive her miraculous dreams. Freeing herself from chaos, she re-creates her vision of the cosmos made of the sensuality of her joyous island and its innocent happiness.

Thérèse, the central character and writing conscience of *Une Forêt pour Zoé*, is in many respects an avatar of Nathalie and Isabelle. Maheux-Forcier keeps certain imagery constant throughout the triptych, so that here again, for example, the flowing mass of luminous hair forms the blazon for each of Thérèse's loves: Zoé, Marie, Mia, and Isis. The tree, strong maple or fragile birch, serves as referent for life or death, security or vulnerability, support or betrayal, courage or cowardice, wisdom or folly. The author's protagonists glide about in an enchanted land filled with evil spells, benevolent charms, disturbing premonitions. Unlike Maheux-Forcier's treatment of earlier incarnations of her heroines, however, considerable emphasis is placed on Thérèse's own powers of astonishment before the world and before the sexual attraction she exerts on others. Her gifts of imagination and invention are no less demanding. The image and theme of flight are reechoed as a primordial need to live a fragmented, contradictory plurality of the self, a need that is also perceived as a danger. Like Nathalie and Isabelle before her, Thérèse adopts false selves by her willingness to please and emulate others whom she loves. In a movement characteristic of Maheux-Forcier's protagonists, Thérèse doubles into and virtually becomes Zoé, Marie, Mia, and Isis; having achieved her new identities, she steps toward another, and secret, existence.

In her conceptualization of the love relationship Thérèse invents scenarios, the aim and essence of which compose, this time, not only a quest for childhood but also a desire to shed the past. Far more than Nathalie and Isabelle, Thérèse is torn between adult sexuality and adolescent sensuality, represented respectively by Isis and Zoé. The truth of Zoé is a rejuvenescence in the eternal; she exemplifies independence from binding ties that compromise the individual self. Refusing imposed social and moral norms, she wills to become impervious to all outside influence. Zoé (childhood) imparts to Thérèse the immediate awareness of the plenitude of the moment, the feeling of having deserved being herself in a privileged corner of the universe, of accepting without guilt the intense satiety of exaltation. Zoé is happiness, Zoé wards off solitude and boredom, Zoé contains the inexplicable and consenting joy of being alive, of knowing the world through a sense of wonder, surprise, and discovery. Zoé pulls Thérèse out of the present, but in so doing draws her back into a past that Maheux-Forcier now views as possibly stark and stiff in death. Obsessed by Zoé-childhood, Thérèse might also be possessed by it, experiencing her adult sexual relationships under the spell of an unsympathetic magic that enslaves her to a long-ago idyllic vision. Indeed, for much of the book Zoé will prevail as the center of time and space, as a symbol of the cult of honesty.

As in the earlier novels, the overwhelming need to preserve the awe of childhood-adolescence is, in good measure, connected to the guilt-inducing tenets of the mother-figure, whose millennial religious prejudices lead her to the belief that sex and happiness are indecencies experienced by natural enemies, that the passage from adolescence to adulthood occurs according to sinful and sinister principles. Hence the larger importance that Maheux-Forcier here lends to the fear of aging, the refusal of the ugly and decrepit in things and beings as monstrous, to the theme of suicide. Hence, too, more forcefully and forthrightly stated than in *Amadou* or *L'Ile joyeuse,* the notions of sensuality as a morality, of a sexuality that would counterbalance and be devoid of guilt and sin. In this respect Isis assumes a pivotal role in the novel, as she is deemed the only adult character fit to know Zoé the child. Isis stands as an appeal against useless reminiscences, despair, and the temptation to suicide. Whereas Zoé represents perfection in sensuality, a happiness permanently locked in upon itself, Isis connotes a pleasure beyond time and consecration. Maheux-Forcier pits her characters in an arena bounded by union and separation, the eternal and the perishable; and, as opposed to her earlier protagonists, Thérèse is able to accept both terms of the dialectics. That perfect happiness does not exist, that the erotic does not eradicate the chaste is, in *Une Forêt pour Zoé,* taken not as a moment of resolution but as a point of departure.

If Maheux-Forcier thinks of her characters as prisoners, she considers them innocent prisoners whose fortunate lot it is to live in a world not fixed by a static past but in a state of perpetual becoming. Like Anne for Nathalie, Zoé is omnipresent in Thérèse's life; the latter bears her childhood anew and as a child-adult confronts the laws of society, its contempts, religious obstacles, and moral conventions, far from daily order and routine. As Zoé did, so Thérèse inextricably links love and friendship. The wisdom of Isis-Zoé further enables Thérèse to rid herself of the guilt of her lesbianism and openly admit the pleasure of homosexual love against the prevailing notion of life as divided into two sexes, organized into families, and justified by the beyond. Maheux-Forcier posits heterosexuality and homosexuality, sensuality and sexuality, as innumerable and reconcilable grays between the extremes of black and white. Thérèse conquers the right to her authenticity as the sole truth; Isis-Zoé gives her the courage to reject a self-betrayal and to accept a truth that, out of a sense of shame for the sexual, appears to adult society as abnormal and sacrilegious. Betrayal consists, furthermore, in possessing rather than offering; and for the author, the sensual experience is the gift of fusing the real and the fantastic, of sharing that enigmatic tenderness and grace of voluptuousness that gives a meaning to life and alone defies absurdity.

Hubert Aquin (1929–1977)

Hubert Aquin, whose suicide was a tragic event for North American literature, stands as one of Quebec's greatest novelists, and his work has elicited a number of exegeses that all seem to converge toward a dialectics of politics versus form, ethics versus aesthetics, the thematics of country versus that of art, with an insistent view upon placing Aquin in the pantheon of autochthonous Quebec commitment literature. While he does, in fact, preach the need for authors to be politically committed, he nonetheless sees this social aspect as inseparable from pure aesthetics. This apparently contradictory stance could, and perhaps should, be considered as an epigraph to all Aquinian writings. *Prochain épisode (Prochain épisode),* 1965, *Trou de mémoire (Blackout),* 1968, and *L'Antiphonaire (The Antiphonary),* 1969, interweave the ethical and aesthetic, the historical and the atemporal, the quotidian and the mythical. Aquin posits the ideal of the creative persona, of individual freedom in terms of the vital thrust inherent in historical evolution, and not as an aestheticism closed in upon itelf and thereby denying the historical moment. For the author, humanism is an open-ended system that necessitates the free exercise of the conscience founded on perception, judgment, and action in opposition to any passive novelistic formalism. The baroque exuberance in Aquin's novels is thus rooted in a totally free interflowing of past, present, and future, in ever-changing geographical space, in chameleon games of realities and symbols and concocted fiction and pseudoautobiography, in the individuality and collectivity of the human condition. These three novels compose vast and convoluted dialogues between the need for social responsibility and the pleasure of the imagining conscience.

Aquin's tantalizingly ambivalent (but not ambiguous) works raise the pivotal question of the evaluative function of spatiotemporal structures in a created construct vis-à-vis its ethics and sociopolitical engagement. The highly elaborate time/space configurations in his novels clearly reflect an influence of France's "New Novelists" of the 1950s and 1960s as they appeal to readers' intellectual responses to a self-generative text unashamedly revealing its creative mechanisms, but they also reflect certain authorial fears of historical links and the risks of freedom.

As with much of contemporary writing, Aquinian fiction is preoccupied, perhaps obsessed with textual processes as such and their autonomous artistic functioning, and it thus incurs the danger of locking its generative powers into the specificity of the text, while depriving it of referential and discursive roles in a larger social context. In point of fact, acute readers of Aquin novels collaborate closely with their author-narrator in organizing and attempting to unravel a multitude of disparate experiences. Far from demolishing the reader's own reality and reducing him to a simple passive object among others that the writer arbitrarily chooses to manipulate, Aquinian time/space wanderings valorize the reader as co-creator—not, however, of an old-style, definitively closed total fiction, but of a totalizing fictionality. This contextual point of view produces mobile, infinitely variable interpretative grids in a text that is a constant state of exploding interactions. *Prochain épisode, Trou de mémoire,* and *L'Antiphonaire,* in their multidimensionality, do not therefore restrict the reader to their formal designs and novelistic techniques, but involve him in endlessly extensible and interchangeable temporal and spatial modes of his and the text's experiential possibilities. Aquin's novels postulate immediate perceptions that in turn provoke divergent complementary or contradictory versions of virtual global qualitative meanings.

Aquinian fiction sets forth a complex network of intra- and transtextual trajectories within sociocultural perspectives but in kaleidoscopic fashion whereby themes, metaphors, and symbols are juxtaposed or superimposed in instants of experience. Traditional linear representational prose becomes an alinear circuit along which actions and reactions, of characters and readers alike, occur in somber zones of potentially dangerous, violent irrationality. It is essential to recall that while Aquin's novels are genially calculated in form and structure (the author obviously attaches considerable importance to game and parody), they never divest his writing of its existential complexity or cathartic function. In Aquin's vision of the universe man can neither fully control inner and outer time and space, nor is he the inescapable victim-figure—he is, rather, acutely aware of certain directions and progressions to which he willingly acquiesces or from which he fearfully retreats. The author refutes the notion of fiction as the necessary reflected image of reality in its unfolding production, order, aim, successiveness; literature does not, nor can it, obey clock temporality or causal intelligibility. Hence the admixture in these novels of purely textual strategies of writing as game, and the subversive tactics of freedom against the terrorism of society. Further, Aquin's novels compose so many diversions of redundancy, dissociation, and doubling, so many metaphors of the author-character-reader's creative processes and social insertion. This mélange of theory and practice, primordial in all three novels, discloses the gratuitous game and the committed gesture that form Aquinian fiction. Aesthetic modalities exist in confluence with sociopolitical ideologies and underscore a basic dilemma in Aquin's entire canon, that is, the author-narrator's refusal of any dichotomization between fiction and myth, the fictitious and the real. All fictions *are* realities, and not simply heuristic excrescences; all human experiences, whether social act or act of writing, are coincidentally confirmed and distorted—and perforce obscure the factual. Therein lies the ubiquitous Aquinian ambivalence: parody and paradox. The stance is, therefore, not equivalent to a negation of all socioethical involvement; neither is it an avowal of fiction as an autocracy to validate highly abstract relational structures expressed in exclusive logical symbolism (time, space, phantasms, simultaneity, and stasis).

In *Prochain épisode, Trou de mémoire,* and *L'Antiphonaire* the novelist moves within a written form of reality that is discretely presentational, rather than consequentially representational in the realist-naturalist tradition—whence situational and characterial overlays and overlaps, and plausible paradoxes that animate a plural relativistic reality. Multiple lines and planes, simultaneously diverse perspectives, bring to Aquin's fiction a virtuosic plasticity, not only in the modes of production, but also in its inscription of certain sociopolitical movements in Quebec. Aquin's novels constitute an unfinished reality, an inexhaustible imagination, for fiction is a means of avoiding what, traditionally, one calls the real world, of creating other worlds; it is an instance of flight and pursuit, of odyssey and quest, of dispossession and alienation, of innocence and liberation. Aquinian narrators, consequently, refuse all oppositional systems in favor of a pluralism that is at once painful and therapeutic, that forms the only credible ontology of collective history and personal conscience.

Prochain épisode's narrator wills an irony and implausibility onto his created text, and similar narratorial arbitrariness occurs in *Trou de mémoire.* The two works promote calculated discontinuity and improvision which rule out the powers of reconstitution according to causality and logic, and underscore the ultimate impotence of appropriating reality. The play of doubles, mirrors, repetitions, redundancy, acquires a privileged status in *Prochain épisode,* a text as space occupied in paginated architecture; the novel's parameters are determined by precisely what it initiates and elaborates, contesting its form and content, multiplying its deliberately contradictory hypotheses, making of the reader an overt connivent partner of narrator and author. As a result, the narrator and reader are aware of being physically within the continuum of textual space as such, whereas the narrators, characters, and readers of traditional realistic-naturalistic novels were localized in representational space. The work consists of rapid-fire peripeteia which short-circuit any straight-line narrative axis by coincidences folding into one another, by an aleatory anecdotal form that points up its own fictivity, by de Quincey's notion that the mind is an immense, complex, and imperishable palimpsest. Each layer only appears to have buried the preceding; in fact, none has been effaced, but rather all layers are forever present, one upon the other. *Prochain épisode'*s narrator-wanderer wills structurations of dispersed psychical and physical time/space comprising fuzzily decipherable, crisscrossing fictional grids. A supralucid narrative "I" roams within the textual space created progressively as the space imposes itself upon the narrator's conscience and as he apprehends it on the level of sensory perception and of imagination.

The importance Aquin attaches to sequence repetition and proliferation focuses attention on the organization mechanisms of *Trou de mémoire,* possibly more than in any of his other novels, and prevents any chronological reconstitution of the book's events and any certitude of the characters' identities. Paradoxically, reconstitution and certitude are favorite pastimes of Aquinian protagonists in his parodistic works. Aquin's willed formalization of space and systematic generation of themes from a limited and severely controlled number of motifs highlight fictional procedures rather than dissimulate them. In *Trou de mémoire* and *L'Antiphonaire* especially Aquin stresses the text as a function of the ensemble of imagined and imaginary forces in their interaction. The multiple narrators of the first of these two works, and narrator Christine Forestier of the second, flagrantly indulge in fabulation as writer, noting that writing, inherently apocryphal, dovetails within the same textual space of fiction and fact, imagination and (auto)biography, novel and diary, plausibility and implausibility.

On the typographical space of the page in *Trou de mémoire* a triple graphic superimposition is effected: upon the character P.X.'s text, an editor (also a character) inscribes his infrapaginal notes; when the narrative "I" shifts in the body of the text from P.X. to the editor, the latter's notes are still appended but now inscribed upon his own text; RR, another character, in the guise of editor also writes her notes on P.X.'s text, or her own, or the "other" editor's, or upon that editor's notes on P.X.'s text in an ongoing game of one-upmanship in writing. The technique of such an intratextuality (letters, diary, [auto]criticism, literary allusions, editorial notes, pastiche, parody) functions by way of microtexts within the global text to scramble narratorial, situational, and characterial data. In a sense, Aquin codes and countercodes his writings to confer an impression of illegibility and non-sense, making of his texts calculated creative articulations of surface phenomena, skeins of narratico-fictional threads spun out into shifting space/time itineraries. Aquinian prose is a domain of waiting and anticipating in improvisation, his narrators are creatures of perception in the present, imagination of the future, and memory of the past in relation to potential futures. Text as space and space as approach to text are concepts of crucial importance in decoding these three novels, or, at least, hypothesizing about them; fiction is trompe l'oeil. The plural anamorphic planes of the text may be known only to one who becomes aware of the angles at which to position himself for looking upon the text. By spatialization of reading itself, by reading obliquely, as it were, according to an anamorphic decoding grid, one is enabled then to grasp fiction as merely possibilities, but in all its possibilities, and all experienced and deciphered in an ultimate simultaneous mix of inner time and mental space.

Aquin subverts the traditional notion of character by multiplying dissociations, duplications, apparent disintegrations accompanied by successive resurrections. Further, the writing subject or imagining conscience is a fictive "I," not responsible for assuming a fiction, but on the contrary created by that fiction. *Prochain épisode*'s narrator proclaims that he is not writing, but being written; in *Trou de mémoire*, P.X., "author," is born through and by words, and the work's "editor" experiences his metamorphosis from a mere editor into a full-fledged writer as he is taken over by the "author" whose work he is editing. Just as a narrator is written by his text, so a character appropriates and directs that narrator's reality, and both are subsumed under the species called reader, who proceeds not to cement the mechanics of the text but to atomize them. In

L'Antiphonaire as well as in the earlier works Aquin displaces the author-to-reader communication wavelength from that of given-message-emanating-from-total-fiction to that of meanings-to-be-questioned-from-open-writing-processes.

In *Trou de mémoire* P.X. Magnant attempts to write an inconceivable novel that would coincide with autobiography, but the work's "editor" character notes P.X.'s deformation of the "true story," which leads the "editor" to complete the narrative by complementary or divergent versions of the events recounted. In the labyrinthine network of pluridimensional planes that compose and decompose *Trou de mémoire,* the character RR appropriates P.X.'s text as her own and denounces the lie of all fiction; having herself assumed P.X. as fictive image, RR will further twist textual plasticity by later denying such authorial identity, claiming it is only a joke, preferring instead to usurp the "editor"'s role and name herself architect of the entire book's order and format.

Aquin's fiction is a game of elucubration set forth by narrator-authors and their various characterial avatars, and often results in humorous parodies of the detective story genre and of innovative techniques of writing in general. *Trou de mémoire*'s creative "I" takes on numerous guises in confluent microtexts in a tongue-in-cheek game of text-on-text, narrator-on-author, author-on-character, narrator-on-character, character-on-narrator, editor-on-author, editor-on-editor—endlessly recycled in fiction that is equally polyvalent characters and situations and the account of those characters and situations. This polyvalence rests upon the notion that "reality" cannot be reducible to a simple univalence, but comports a multiplicity of mobiles doubling into the subject reflecting itself and the object reflected.

While *L'Antiphonaire* blends concerns about Quebec political commitment and statements on contemporary North American civilization, it is essentially a text of parodistic perspectives. Its themes reproduce various commonplace novelistic traditions; its styles run the gamut from rhetorical bombast to pseudosurrealistic imagery. But what is, again here, singularly striking about the novel is Aquin's inscription of the problematics of writing into textuality itself. That is, writing is the act that generates the text as, specifically, the object of writing, and not as a literary fact constituting an identifiable authorial psychology, or sociohistorical panoply, or moralizing vision. The written word occupies space, volume, and time, which contour their autonomous structural realities. *L'Anti-phonaire* is at once auto-production (text pointing to its own textuality, commenting upon its multiplicative modalities) and anti-production (consciously parodistic in articulating links to other literary genres and in elaborating ironic levels of discourse—medical, academic, philosophic, poetic, moral, aesthetic), and these two modes set up a highly stereotyped distance in the relationship between author and reader, as between author and himself. The novel is a collage of various narrative-discursive techniques that both structure the entire work and destroy all aesthetic systems by assuming them in parodic fashion. Rather than have definitive recourse to any inner moral or psychological truth or to any exterior sociological or political reality, *L'Antiphonaire*'s language and writing reflect upon themselves in their own shifting economy.

Aquin's writing forms a deliberate break in the conventions of the novelistic tradition, and it also ruptures its particular literarity by constantly constructing and deconstructing character identities and spatiotemporal referents. In *L'Antiphonaire* the author inscribes onto the book's time/space palimpsests (the Italian Renaissance and the contemporary North American continent) bourgeois, capitalist culture codes, materialism and servile ideological language which he parodies and caricatures. In this novel parody is an active subversion of all themes, the work being turned upon itself in a gesture that both embodies and voids it. Irony transforms themes from usually hidden novelistic devices, propelling the text forward, into overt fictional processes, fragmenting the text and distancing the reader from it. Referents of Aquin's parody are, for instance, types of characters or modes of protagonists (the Tragic Heroine, the Unscrupulous Stranger, the Rejected Mistress, the Guilt-Ridden Adulteress, the Perpetrator of Calamity), literary genres (suspense, detective, adventure writings, melodrama, the French "New Novel"), sociocultural archetypes.

In *L'Antiphonaire* Aquin activates the parody/caricature process through its basic dynamics of deformation, by hyperbole or antiphrasis, on the levels of both fiction and narration. The reader often finds himself addressed directly and attacked as an unwitting, disbelieving bystander, at one remove from what he is being forced to witness. The recurring apostrophic reference to the "dear reader" serves to explode the conventional identification between narrator-character and reader by this willed estrangement that deconditions the reader. As in earlier Aquin novels, *L'Antiphonaire*'s narrator-author is a mercurially chamelionlike creature for whom the novel is an apocryphal text, reality is an atomized vision, writing is polarized into irreconcilable opposites, and the writer is an extravagant fragmentalist. Christine Forestier, one alias among several, as the book's narrator-author, catalogues the numerous doubles she alternately or simultaneously assumes throughout the work, and at the same time reveals by accusation the apocrypha by or about them, speaking of her shattered prose, of defocalized reality. Aquin's antiphonally grafted passages, concepts, and schema are in the manner of textual puzzles, the novel mocking itself for its overabundance of unverifiable historical references. The redundant use of capsule plot recapitulations (often as deliberately awkward parenthetical interpolations) effectively demythifies fictional truth and reality by exposing the logistics of fictionality. Christine admits her incongruous, blurred narrative mode and her mock-critical discussions of written transpositions of Truth, and avows her preference for the possibilities of off-focus images inherent in the filmic process.

Aquin constantly dephases reality; Christine as narrator-author discovers the phase displacement between herself and realities surrounding her, between herself and her lover, viewed as a character, between herself and herself. Dephasing also occurs in character and situation reversals, or when Aquin short-circuits his fiction by over-obvious, superfluous textual addenda: documentary information in the midst of orgasmic violence; cosmic irony shattering a melodramatic event; medical or academic modes of discourse juxtaposed with lyrico-poetic modes. The multiple scripts of *L'Antiphonaire* comprise exercises in textual extrapolations, calculated (im)probable hypotheses in which Aquin caricatures the sacrosanct rules of verisimilitude: nothing is impossible, but all possibilities remain mere possibilities, and as such are questionable, unreliable, speculative.

By inventorying into *L'Antiphonaire* a substantial core of bourgeois ideology (general morality, conjugal happiness, maternity/paternity, career, prestigious success), Aquin attacks it in burlesque, iconoclastic episodes of sexuality and violence, adultery and abortion, failure and shame. The novel is thus a game of transgression of conventional literary production and dominant ideology, but it is also a game of imitation; the parodistic process contains within itself its own double (duality or duplicity?) for it is a dialectics of both reference and difference, the text existing simultaneously with the parodying scripts and the parodied components. Aquin's novels are, therefore, not to be read literally but as dialogues of suspicion, alternating between conformity to the literature and ideology observable in the texts and a deformity of that literature and ideology by parody, caricature, and irony.

Marie-Claire Blais (1939–   )

Marie-Claire Blais's works explore troubled worlds, disturbing characters, situations that range from the vaguely unpleasant to the utterly hopeless. On occasion there are traces of humor, but even these seem grimly determined, while a certain in-spite-of-all-odds optimism can appear to be unrealistic fantasizing. Blais seeks in her writings to promote an acceptance of marginal, or tormented, or alienated characters for whom the author sometimes expresses solicitude and pity dangerously close to the bathetic. Within their fictional world these characters are often misunderstood, unloved, or badly loved. Certain types recur with obsessive frequency from novel to novel: the suicide; the young boy dying of a fatal disease; the male or female prostitute; the criminal. Equally prevalent are the personages who derive their raison d'être from their (often ineffectual) efforts to alleviate the sufferings of others. Self-sacrifice and dedication provoked by inner angst prove to be particularly inappropriate methods for trying to earn love. Blais's pessimism is not total, however. Though there exist situations of unloving mothers and intense sibling rivalries, in other instances one finds the exact opposite. While romantic love as pictured offers more obstacles than satisfactions to the protagonists, they are often aware of other couples' happiness, some of whom persist in believing in love as an ideal, and many characters find a greater or lesser measure of happiness in creativity and the arts.

Blais's earliest novels had already drawn the attention and praise of important critics when, at the age of twenty-six, her *Une Saison dans la vie d'Emmanuel (A Season in the Life of Emmanuel),* 1965, established her as a major writer and won international renown. The novel relates a brief period in the life of the infant Emmanuel's family; from the working class, poverty-stricken, it is dominated by Grandmother Antoinette, who commands the reader's admiration through her courage, her belief in education, her love for Jean le Maigre (Skinny John), her exemplary common sense, and her lucid intelligence concerning the milieu in which she lives. At the same time it is obvious that her method of maintaining her power, her open conflicts with the children's father, her total overshadowing of the mother are of a sort to traumatize a family psychologically for untold generations. Unlike André Gide, Blais does not proclaim her hatred of families, but neither has she yet depicted a lovable or even a healthy one. Fathers, in particular, fail to provide support for and security of love to their children. When they are not entirely absent, they are weaklings, opposed to the education their creative children so ardently desire, sometimes completely absorbed in their own usually frustrated homosexuality, or, at best, simply inadequately able to love and accept others.

Most of the family's members remain uncharacterized. Interest centers essentially on Jean le Maigre, with peripheral attention paid to the brothers closest to him in age, Pomme (Apple—or, Potato) and Le Septième (the Seventh), and to one older sister, Héloïse. Blais uses Pomme as an illustration of the horrors of poverty, when, sent to work in a factory as a child, he loses his fingers in an accident to which his elders are mostly indifferent. Le Septième, Jean's partner in childhood debaucheries and dreams, represents other kinds of victimization: attacks by sadistic children, lack of adult understanding, seemingly benevolent attentions from a perverted ex-monk; yet he reacts forcefully against the evil that confronts him. Jean, nonetheless, prophesies that Le Septième will end up on the scaffold. Héloïse, on the other hand, is given to ecstasies that underscore the recognized interaction between sensuality and mysticism. Expelled from a convent, she finds her true vocation in The Inn of the Public Rose, a bordello managed by the golden-hearted Octavie Enbonpoint (Stout Octavia). Jean le Maigre himself is a richly varied mixture of virtues and vices. Sexually active (first with his brothers, later with coseminarians), an arsonist, thief, and liar, he spends time in a reformatory. Nevertheless, he reveals aspects of saintliness in his compassion; he faces imminent death from tuberculosis without fear and even with a certain intellectual curiosity; shows a well-developed sense of the incongruous, the humorous, the absurd; and is a precociously creative writer. Like a majority of intellectuals of her generation in Quebec, Blais is often selectively anticlerical without being opposed to religion per se. The novel's devil-figure, the complete villain, is Brother Théodore Crapula (Dissolute Theodore), who takes pleasure in and hastens the death of his monastery's young seminarians. Other members of religious orders as well as the priest-hood appear as less than holy and grievously lacking in love for their fellow humans.

While *Une Saison dans la vie d'Emmanuel* bears upon virtually every theme around which the author articulates most of her books, the work avoids numerable pitfalls of subsequent novels, mainly because of the author's great sympathy for her characters and their plights. Themes that elsewhere elicit embarrassingly maudlin passages or occasionally hortatory didacticism are rendered objectively here, their power being in no wise diminished thereby. Moreover, the ironic distance with which Blais delineates her characters poses no hin-drance to the reader's involvement but allows for a considerable amount of the humor of self-recognition. The energy and strength of Jean's creativity, of Le Septième's revolt, of Héloïse's generous sexuality, and of nearly every facet of Grandmother Antoinette's existence ensure that the forces of life in the book far outweigh its negativity.

Blais's *Manuscrits de Pauline Archange (Manuscripts of Pauline Ar-change)*, 1968, *Vivre! Vivre!* (part two of *Manuscripts of Pauline Ar-change*), 1969, and *Les Apparences (Dürer's Angel)*, 1970, form a trilogy under the collective title of the first of the three and purport to be the autobiography of Pauline Archange, recounting significant portions of the protagonist's childhood and adolescence, and her fundamental desire both to transcend and to immortalize her ne-cessitous existence by writing about it. As a narrational device this optics eventually subverts itself: by assuming the passage of many years since the occurrence of the events in question, we can excuse the narrator for projecting adult sentiments and judgments into what are presented as a child's reactions, but that are beyond the scope of the most precocious child. However, other segments of the narrative dealing with the lives and feelings of some of the secondary characters cannot be accounted for as realities known to Pauline, hence the necessity of positing an omniscient writer (who may or may not be Pauline) of fictions that may or may not include Pauline herself.

Recurrent Blaisian themes define Pauline's world: disease and death, humiliation, economic exploitation, alcoholism, insanity, a constant frustrating of even the most modest ambitions. Kindness and forgiveness (toward marginal figures—a prostitute, a murderer) are offset by unsparing criticism of members of religious establishments who, out of a distorted sense of shame and fear, deny basic bodily realities, and by criticism of parental brutality and terror. Not atypically, Blais imbues some of the novel's more complex figures with a curious ambiguity. Doctor Germaine Léonard, while devoting her working life to aiding the indigent, exhibits an insensitivity and class-consciousness that condemn everything in Pauline that marks her as one of the working-class poor. The Franciscan Benjamin Robert incarnates both pure evil, in his sexual abuse of Pauline, and pity and commiseration for the murderer Philippe L'Heureux in whose defense against Doctor Léonard's condemnation he becomes a savior-figure.

The trilogy offers ample proof of Blais's talents as a master of the brief, vivid character sketch in addition to the fuller development of her protagonist. Pauline's childhood love for Séraphine; her feelings of guilt for loving unsubstantially in some of the work's pivotal situations; her sensitivity to the deficiencies in her education; her gratitude for the love she receives from others, as insufficient as it too may be; and especially her hopes and efforts to become a writer— these elements combine to make Pauline Archange one of Blais's most sharply etched and memorable characters.

Le Loup (The Wolf), 1972, expands Blais's usual cast of characters and, like other works, revolves around sensuality and, specifically, assumed or repressed homosexuality. Upon several extended metaphors the novel builds a quasi-mystical parable of Sébastien's largely frustrated quest for sanctity, while ostensibly telling in his own words the history of his multiple loves and adventures. The all-pervading image is that of hunger and nourishing, with its corollaries of thirst and providing drink. Closely connected are the figures of the lamb and the wolf (whence the title), but this metaphor adds the notion of ferocious voracity on the part of him who hungers, and passive acceptance and sacrifice from the one who is seen as actively nourishing. The negative image of the judge as condemner is linked with that of the wolf, while the healer is associated with the nourisher.

Sébastien's liaisons offer prototypes of love as Blais usually portrays it. Truly successful couples, of whatever sexuality, are never central characters in her works, but rather are seen occasionally as background figures, and as such are represented as enviable, but also as living a fragile, danger-fraught existence, potential victims of boredom, deception, shattering of illusions, or the death of one of the partners. It is a constant in the Blaisian corpus that love relationships are imbalanced, one lover always disproportionately giving and conceding, while the other unconcernedly merely takes. But neither giving nor taking ever seems to involve total commitment, and couplings develop with the clear implication of their eventual dissolution. As their existence reaches its term, the "lamb" finds that he too has been in many ways nourished by the "wolf." Though Sébastien, in drawing up his autobiography, senses that he may have accomplished no more than awakening the appetites of those he sought to succor and heal, though he may have failed to show requisite affection and have been incapable of others' redemption, though each affair has ended in sterility, still he concludes that the effort to attain and realize a deep and lasting human rapport must continue to be the aim of his life.

Les Nuits de l'Underground (Nights in the Underground: An Exploration of Love), 1978, at times a tractlike apology for homosexual love, derives its title from a lesbian bar called the "Underground," a name deliberately laden with symbolism. Another rather too patently obvious and hackneyed symbol is that of seasonal cycles. A brief affair marked by one partner's refusal to allow another to penetrate her inner solitude and unwillingness to relinquish her promiscuity begins and ends in winter. In spring the character transcends her emotional pain, and her artistic creativity blossoms; as the book closes, in summer, another character triumphantly announces that the time of the Underground is over, the moment of freedom has arrived. The book is rampant with inordinate physical and psychological suffering, abounds in images of enslavement, captivity, cages, traps, prisons; many of the female characters have been abused, or abandoned, or repressed, or otherwise hurt by particular men as well as by male-dominated society in general (by an ironic quirk, in the lesbian aesthetics of the novel, "virile" and "masculine" are terms of praise when applied to a woman). More than in any other novel Blais makes abundant use of an awkward, artificial English, justified when Lali the Austrian speaks it, for she is said to have difficulties still with both English and French, but several Canadian and American characters intercalate English into their conversations in regrettably stilted ways. The author, obviously, wishes to investigate certain key themes: the isolation of the individual, the impossibility and undesirability of love-as-possession, the role of art as the sole means of authentic communication;

but, in final analysis, her "exploration of love" is insubstantial and unconvincing.

Themes of noncommunication, suffering, and anomie form the nucleus of Blais's *Le Sourd dans la ville (Deaf to the City),* 1979, quite possibly her richest and best-realized work to date. Deafness and blindness, figurative rather than literal, become powerful symbols of alienation, as characters fail to listen, refuse to see, and remain apathetic to the pain that surrounds them. The novel's primary optics is that of a middle-aged woman, connoisseur of art, deserted by her husband, and a keen observer of the tenants of the fleabag hotel she has chosen as the setting for her suicide. Florence represents an extreme case of the perils posed by resignation of individual autonomy in favor of the couple. Prior to her death, with which the book reaches its close, she reflects upon the years of her marriage and remembers various couples, heterosexual and homosexual, whom she has known and who appear to have found ways of coping with life and its multitudinous obstacles and enigmas.

The hotel dwellers include familiar, obsessive Blaisian types: a young boy in the throes of a fatal illness who serves as one of the novel's suffering savior-figures; his sister, a young prostitute and victim of society and its systems, a victim especially of poverty and a total lack of encouragement for developing her finer instincts, who follows in the path traced by their mother; an older sister who has cut herself off completely from the family, hopes to achieve respectability through education, but feels overwhelming guilt, aloneness, and a sense of impending failure and rejection. The nourishing Great Mother figure who runs the Hotel des Voyageurs, in addition to tending to her work as dancer and sex object, functions as another of Blais's suffering saviors: the dream that she instills in her dying son of their forthcoming trip to the flowering and restorative desert invests the book with some of its most beautiful and moving passages.

The one character who is truly troubled by and working to alleviate individual as well as universal suffering is the philosophy teacher, Judith Langenais. Blais makes of her an allegorical figure, referred to usually as Judith Lange (Judith the Angel), and uses her as the essential vehicle for articulating the author's own preoccupations with violence and misery, ranging from Nazi concentration camps and the Vietnam war, to abandoned and slaughtered animals,

to humans in need of sadomasochistic relationships in order to function as personal and social beings.

In *Visions d'Anna (Anna's World)*, 1982, the author's characterial
incarnations of various social and psychological questions reappear,
but often obliquely, as perceived by encounters or readings experienced by the characters rather than as happening to the characters
whom the reader knows directly. At the heart of the book is the
image of drifting away, caught up by forces that one neither com-
prehends nor controls, and of an eventual, if ill-defined return.
Anna leaves home while an adolescent, wanders the world, and in
time returns to the room she had known as a child, only to indulge
there in obsessive visions of various forms of apocalypse. The novel
ends on a note of forced optimism and bitter pessimism not infrequently heard in Blais's works. The reader is told that Anna's visions
have ended, but Anna herself realizes that if she does, indeed, return
to the world she must thereby inevitably become a participant in
humanity's crimes; in the Blaisian vision freedom and belonging
seem, of necessity, intertwined with bondage and alienation.

Réjean Ducharme (1941–   )

Réjean Ducharme's writings exhibit many of the preoccupations
found in Marie-Claire Blais's fiction. The two writers are admirers
of each other's work, and each has dedicated a novel to the other.
In their respective books poverty-stricken characters are acutely conscious of being insufficiently loved; further, there recur delinquency,
alcoholism, child abuse, suicide, death of children, social rejection.
Blais's and Ducharme's central personages are all wounded to the
core, and yet, in spite of so many similarities, the principal concerns
and modes of reactions expressed in the two novelistic productions
differ significantly. The typical Blaisian character responds to the
evils of society and the pain of individual existence with compassion,
an attempt at understanding, introspection, often with a certain
amount of self-pity or resignation, and not uncommonly by expecting personal suffering to furnish either the catalyst or the materials for artistic creativity. Ducharme's protagonists, by contrast,
rebel actively, openly, or violently, identify competitors and seek
to eliminate them, scorn and lash out at those who offend them.
Blais's characters try to justify and condone the shortcomings of

others, whereas Ducharme's condemn out-of-hand the general mediocrity of the universe at large.

Ducharme's works display dazzling verbal inventiveness, which some critics have seen as a form of revolt against the limits of language and the societal norms represented by language. The very titles of the novels are untranslatable plays on words; and the distortions of accepted language and spelling, as well as an overriding interest in onomastics underscored by punning peculiarities in naming, abound in every story and on virtually every page. Bérénice Einberg, the narrator of *L'Avalée des avalés* (*The Swallower Swallowed*), 1966, goes so far as to create a new language in order to express her hatred for and refutation of adults. Words are used as weapons throughout the author's canon.

The theme of childhood, the privileged moment of existence, occupies the foreground of the entire Ducharme corpus; his first works, indeed, feature children or adolescents as their protagonists. Though the principal characters are older in the later *La Fille de Christophe Colomb* (Christopher Columbus's daughter), 1969, *L'Hiver de force* (*Wild to Mild: A Tale*), 1973, and *Les Enfantômes* (The ghosts of childhood; play on *enfants*, children, and *fantômes*, phantoms), 1976, they retain an abundant number of traits normally considered to be childlike, and are enchanted by the memories of what they have been. The early novels are, at least to a certain extent, built about stories of initiation, the dilemmas of growing up, of coming to grips with the real and mediocre world of adults, a world that Bérénice repels from the beginning to the end. Her narrative traces the transformation of an intelligent, imaginative but frustrated child into a monstrously cynical adolescent, living and considering herself as an adult, yet repulsed by her body, by love, even friendship, and the universe in general. Her sense of inferiority twists into delusions of grandeur as she views herself to be some kind of evil cosmic force. Her loathing of others reflects but another aspect of her self-hatred, while her need to escape from the anxieties aroused by her feelings of solitude and rejection, as well as by the existential realities of time, sexuality, and ultimate death, pushes her toward the illogical desire for death—hers and others'. Trapped in a destiny that inspires her with horror, she attempts to flee from mediocrity by repudiating all similarity with fellow humans, at the same time denying all responsibility for her own being.

Mille Milles, the protagonist of *Le Nez qui voque* (Equivocation; play on *nez*, nose, and *équivoque*), 1967, the least voluntaristic, the only male, and the most conscious of self as narrator/writer among the principal characters of Ducharme's earliest novels, is equally the one most aware of his clinging to childhood and his eventual acceptance of adulthood. For over two-thirds of the book he tries to arrest his development, struggles to repress his sexuality, decries the progress of technology, and plans to avoid maturity by dying first. But then, suspecting the deceptiveness of words and their inadequacy to translate reality, he turns from his definitions of childhood as equal to beauty and innocence, of adulthood as ugliness, compromise, disgust and despair, and instead embraces life with its manifold possibilities of change and growth. The book strikes, nevertheless, a darker note. Chateaugué, the unloved orphan who was Mille Milles's friend and with whom he had had a suicide pact, proceeds to kill herself, an act that some critics have chosen to interpret as symbolic of the death of Mille Milles's youth.

L'Océantume (An ocean of bitterness; play on *océan, mer*, sea, and *amertume*, bitterness), 1968, presents a similar duality; the energetic and joyful little girl, Iode Ssouvie, is the narrator and principal character whose enthusiasm is all-inclusive, ranging from a delight in verbal delirium to recognition of the rewards of friendship, of sexuality, of travel. Contrasted with Iode's vitality and strength are the lack of distinction and the baseness of certain adults. Mediocrity is, for example, embodied in Faire Faire Desmains, a ridiculous woman who desires to remain a child; on the other hand, York epitomizes cruelty as a cattleman whose starving gaurs are saved through the heroic efforts of Iode and her companion Asie Azothe.

Ducharme's three latest books—this immensely talented writer has not published a novel since 1976, though he has continued to work in other genres—are articulated around adults rather than children; nonetheless, the interest in childhood has not disappeared. *La Fille de Christophe Colomb*, a novel composed entirely in self-mocking verse, most of it rhymed, unfolds in the realm of sheer fantasy the story of Colombe Colomb. Although her own childhood is encompassed in only a few pages, she becomes a kind of surrogate mother to thousands of animals and displays the same sort of enthusiasm as Iode Ssouvie. Her tale is suffused with an ambience of bawdiness and irreverence (God, e.g., appears under the name of Al Capone), and yet, beneath the lighthearted story and the wordplay, it is possible to discern serious social and political problems, including disparities in the wealth of nations, the hypocrisy of labor unions, the menace of nuclear destruction, with many a passing jibe at the United States for its smugness derived from its advanced technology.

The male and female protagonists of *L'Hiver de force* are in the process of living banality to its extreme limits, a passive rebellion against all bourgeois values. Their daily existence consists of watching television, smoking, talking about movies and records, drinking beer, avoiding their landlord because they are in arrears, and occasionally taking on work which will enable them to pursue their directionless life. Ducharme's typical linguistic virtuosity surfaces in the notebooks of André Ferron, the narrator who is ultraconscious of writing qua writing. André and his companion Nicole realize their infatuation with the children they once were; they are still childlike, if not patently childish, in their shrugging off any sense of responsibility, and in their attachment to and need for Petit Pois, a famous actress, who acts as a surrogate mother to the couple.

Vincent Falardeau's narrative in *Les Enfantômes* nostalgically conjures up that "immaterial island" that is the past shared by Vincent and his sister, Fériée. Vincent pens this memoir after Fériée's death, a suicide like their mother's. Fériée, in part an extension of the mother-figure for Vincent, becomes, through the book's imagery, both the writer's creation (she is his "little leaf," evoking the relationship of the leaf to the branch, but also that of the writer and the pages of his work) and his native country. In this capacity she serves as the counterpart of Vincent's wife, Alberta, emblem of the anglophone culture that he has embraced, betraying thus his own past and assuring an incompatible and unhappy marriage. On one level, then, *Les Enfantômes* is Ducharme's most overtly political novel, yet its politics could yield multiple interpretations. Is there guilt for not preserving a past that in any case has determinedly persisted in its own annihilation? Is there recognition that an isolated francophone Quebec culture *must* be relegated to the past, that it is only in collaboration with the anglophone culture, however mismatched the union, that the present and the future are possible? Or does the book deny and denounce that alliance, positing the revivification of the past, through art if not in life, as the sole path to fulfillment?

All Ducharme's novels (like his screenplay for *Les Bons Débarras,* [Good riddance]) revolve either around children or around adults who reveal qualities generally associated with children, and who tend to idealize childhood. The works show, moreover, a single dominant psychological pattern in the theme of the child's inability to establish a satisfactory relationship with its mother. Time and again, the central characters are abandoned, neglected, or loved in such a manner that their need for love remains ungratified. Questa, mother to three daughters of her own and surrogate mother to Mille Milles and Chateaugué, is an alcoholic. Mme Einberg, Ina Ssouvie, and the *poule* (here, "prostitute"), Colombe's mother, are alcoholic and adulterous, while "La Toune" (a highly negatively charged term in Quebec speech), the mother-figure for André and Nicole, is promiscuous and addicted to drugs. The real mothers and the mother-figures alike reject their children in not a few ways. Mme Einberg and Ina Ssouvie both love another sibling more than the child who is the protagonist. Man (telescoped pronunciation of *maman*) Falardeau, by her suicide, leaves her small children motherless; Questa frequently deserts her daughters at night. Ina runs away from home, and although she is eventually reunited with Iode, she meets a premature death in a separately published continuation of *L'Océantume* (*"Fragment inédit de* l'Océantume"). There are other such abandonments by death: Colombe's mother is killed because of the scandal she provokes; Chateaugué is an orphan; Nicole and André recall the anniversary of the mother's death—whether André's or Nicole's is not made clear, but the two characters are so basically identified with each other that the question has little importance.

The long-dead mother pales in significance, however, when compared with the role that "La Toune" plays in Nicole's and André's life, and the same dynamics marks their relationship with her that defines child-mother rapports in the author's other works. They adore her, want to possess her completely, and live in constant fear lest their longings become too obvious and alienate her. She alternates between excessively effusive affection for them and near-total or total neglect. The novel ends as she severs her relation with them, assuring them that she loves them too much to be able to endure being with them on occasion only.

On a different level Ducharme's novels can be said to have the act and the result of writing as their central subject. In every work the writing constantly calls attention to itself, often by deliberate orthographical distortions, by the use of joual, anglicisms, slang, puns, and spoonerisms, by taking figurative expressions literally, by veritable deluges of accumulations, by extraordinary names freighted with meaning given to so many of the characters, by comparisons so prosaic as to disconcert. And yet the total mood turns poetic, creating often a delicate, dreamlike, evanescent space, devolving wholly in the realm of imagination and fantasy. These lexical gymnastics prolong a tradition in French letters represented by, among others, such diverse authors as François Rabelais, Lautréamont, Alfred Jarry, Raymond Queneau, Boris Vian, Eugène Ionesco, and J.M.G. Le Clézio.

It is not merely on the linguistic and semantic levels that the writing is deictic and self-conscious, but on that of narrative as well, with numerous direct and indirect references to other authors and other works. All the novels, with the exception of *La Fille de Christophe Colomb,* are first-person narratives. The early *L'Avalée des avalés* and *L'Océantume* with female protagonists differ from the three with males at their center (*Le Nez qui voque, L'Hiver de force,* and *Les Enfantômes*) in that the latter call the readers' attention to themselves not only as actors in the events of the story, but also as writers of the text being produced. That is, the evidence seems to indicate that the choice of sex for the principal character exerts a powerful influence here on the level of author/personage identification. These novels refer repeatedly to the text in the process of being created— the type of paper used, the ink with which it is written, the date on which the author stares at the blank sheets, the room, the lighting. Such purely physical details remind readers constantly of the text as writing, and of their own role as receptors of that text. Ducharme incorporates other facets of the thematics of writing per se into the fictional world being depicted. At the very outset of *L'Hiver de force* André decides to record his and Nicole's existence as a release from a dead-end situation. Mille Milles, afraid to speak directly with others, declares that he prefers the written word as a mode of communication. Vincent writes as a means of "escaping from generalized disgust," as a plunge into the abyss of his emotions in order to rescue the memory of his past, symbolized by Fériée, from encroaching oblivion.

These three narrators comment on their style and criticize the fruit of their invention. The effect, paradoxically, renders the novelistic universe with its narrator/author less realistic and underlines the omnipresence of Ducharme, manipulating every component of the text. In *Les Enfantômes* the distancing is at its most pronounced, for the author interjects himself, not as a fiction but as reality, signing his initials into a final note describing Vincent's memoirs as written in an attic by the light of a candle stuck into a Seven-Up bottle. The narrator represents a caricature of the writer, just as the text itself, in spite of the seriousness of so much of its subject matter, provides by its insistent word games a parody of literature. Through comedy and irony the writer can both produce examples of sincere emotions, characters to whom he is attached, attitudes that echo his own, and a literary genre that he appreciates; and, at the same time, he can detach himself from them, and thus protect his deeper feelings from possible criticisms or attacks.

Roch Carrier (1937–   )

Roch Carrier has written poems, short stories, and plays, but most of his creative energies have been devoted to the novel. His initial work in that genre, *La Guerre, yes sir! (La Guerre, Yes Sir!)*, 1968, confirmed him as a major talent and became an immediate best-seller. The first work of a trilogy titled "Somber Times," it is set in a small Quebec community during World War II. The action centers around the wake held for young Corriveau, a soldier killed when he steps on a mine in France, whose body, accompanied by a cortege of seven English soldiers, is returned home for burial. In burlesque manner the story satirizes, but not without affection, the life, attitudes, and provincialism of the village's inhabitants, as well as the enormous cultural gap between them and the English soldiers.

The soldiers display all the traits typical of a Quebec caricature of the English as sober, disciplined, condescending, Protestant, gloomy, dull. They in turn conclude that Quebecers are swine, intractable, undisciplined, solitary, fearful, rather unintelligent, not gifted for any of the traditional professions, less civilized than the Indians, whereas, if they had only been willing to become English, England would have civilized them and brought them a civilized language rather than their patois. With none of the soldiers nor the villagers capable of translating more than the most rudimentary words and phrases, the situation is set for all possible quid pro quos.

Carrier accentuates the comic potential by his broad caricature of the villagers, portrayed as earthy, bawdy, ignorant, egoistic, hot-tempered, violent at times—but also generous, hospitable, fun-loving, and life-embracing. Even as Carrier multiplies the scenes of pure farce, a serious political stance becomes evident. The author casts his sympathies with those who choose life over death, who may resign themselves to the inevitable, but who will withstand oppression as long as resistance offers any chance of success; with the small in their opposition to the mighty; and obviously, with his francophone Quebecers forced by the dominant anglophones to fight and die in a war they do not understand, defending a flag they do not recognize, a cause that, at least to a certain extent, represents their own subjugation.

The political theme, however, never overwhelms the work, and interest centers on the humor, on Carrier's ability to create memorable, surrealist tableaux—a scene such as that in which one of Corriveau's sisters, bound by religious vows not to enter the family home again, stands praying for her brother beside an open window while the mourners kneel around the coffin in the suddenly glacial house, then disappears again through the night and snow—on the remarkably natural-seeming dialogue (though, in truth, perfectly controlled artistically), the powerful visual evocations, and on the wide range of emotions that the author elicits in the reader.

Floralie, où es-tu? (Floralie, Where Are You?), 1969, the second novel of the trilogy, recedes a generation in time to relate the tale of the beginning of married life for Anthyme and Floralie Corriveau (parents of the dead soldier in *La Guerre, yes sir!*) as they are about to set out for their own home just after their wedding and ending at dawn the following morning. Their first sexual encounter leads Anthyme to believe, rightly, that Floralie is not a virgin. He strikes her, walks away, and for the rest of the night they are separated from each other. Alternating sections of the text then recount their individual wanderings through a forest, their thoughts and emotions, and their encounter with a panoply of mysterious archetypal beings, encounters that ultimately enable them to struggle through to a reconciliation with their situation and with each other.

Carrier's ability to create vivid, sometimes surreal scenes comes again to the fore, and many could be cited as masterpieces of their kind: the description of a runaway horse; several of the scenes with Néron, the traveling medicine man and his children, who decorate their Christmas tree with living mice; evocations of visits by the devil to carry sinners off to Hell; descriptions of the troup of actors who enlist Floralie to represent the Virgin Mary in their play about the seven deadly sins; and the entire section concerning Father

Nombrillet, the gathering for the festival of the Holy Thorn, and the ensuing holocaust. As the book closes, the reader becomes aware that the forest has been the dark night of the soul, and the creatures have existed merely in the couple's dreams. In *Floralie, où es-tu?* Carrier displays his talent as a humorist only from time to time, but his mastery of description and dialogue, his keen sense of observation, and his ability to breathe life into his characters in just a few lines remain constantly evident.

Il est par là, le soleil (Is It the Sun, Philibert?), 1970, the concluding part of the trilogy, is much darker in tone than its predecessors. Near the end of *La Guerre, yes sir!* Philibert, son of the brutal Arsène, upon being told that he is now a man, walks away, never to return to his native village. *Il est par là, le soleil* tells the story of Philibert's life in Montreal and terminates when he dies in an automobile accident. Like *Floralie, où es-tu?*, this work can be considered the story of a rite of passage. But whereas Floralie and Anthyme successfully complete their initiation and are thus ready to assume their role as adults in the society for which they have been prepared, the immature Philibert, attempting integration into an unknown environment, must inevitably fail, and the result is tragedy. The title of the trilogy as a whole is thereby accounted for: by considering the three books together, we see the oft-treated hard but happy traditional life in Quebec giving way to a period of contact with and curiosity about the world beyond, and ending with the disaster that befalls when all the old values are abandoned. By exploiting this vein of nostalgia for the simpler pleasures of Quebec's rural past, Carrier gives yet another example of what is probably the single most important recurring motif in Quebec literature.

Il est par là, le soleil opens with a series of anecdotes concerning Philibert's life, first during his village years, later in Montreal. Several of them further illustrate Carrier's gift of evoking powerful emotions, a sense of mystery and wonder, and striking visualization; the novel shows again his sense of humor. Unlike the two earlier works of the trilogy, however, this novel's many tales do not revolve around any central event. The work lacks a sense of time, and many of the incidents are but variant versions of the same basic scenario: Philibert, holding one menial job after another, realizes that life should consist of something better, and repeatedly quits his work, while declaiming his independence and his revolt. The multiplication of such incidents follows no particular progression (though

Carrier renders a few of them memorable through some especially unusual detail, however implausible), and the redundancy diminishes the potential for effectiveness. Judicious editing would no doubt have modified or eliminated several passages embarrassing by reason of their banality, their naiveté, their melodramatics, or, as in the description of Philibert's fatal accident, their excessive length.

Carrier has a flair for depicting characters, but, for the most part, he does not give them a sense of development through time, and in this respect Philibert is no exception. He neither learns nor grows in any noticeable way. Events, including his inheriting what seems to him a fortune and his eventual death, are not necessitated by his character, nor do they derive from any discernable inner logic in the novel, but rather they spring arbitrarily from the author's whims. By structuring each of his other novels treated here around a single central event, Carrier avoids the principal weakness of *Il est par là, le soleil.*

With *Le Deux-millième Etage (They Won't Demolish Me!),* 1973, Carrier returns to the essentially comic style and preoccupations of his first novel, but the setting is the willingly assumed contemporary urban landscape of Montreal. The theme of ineffectual revolt, as so often in Carrier's work, generates the plot. The characters, like those of *La Guerre, yes sir!,* are predominantly one-dimensional caricatures whose stories intertwine as a result of their being neighbors and sharing a common problem. In this instance, they all live in Dorval's rooming house, scheduled to be demolished to make room for a skyscraper apartment building. Dorval mobilizes his motley and marginal tenants in the battle to save his house, emblematic for him of the larger class struggle of the weak against the strong, the small entrepreneur against the anonymous and brutish forces of bureaucracy and capitalism. The novel's rich ironies appear as the various characters, including Dorval himself, prove only too eager to enjoy the benefits of capitalist society. Dorval, left alone in his struggle, gives up and abandons the house to its destruction when a bulldozer operated by two of his former tenants arrives.

Le Deux-millième Etage, using many of the same comic techniques, several analogous characters, and certain of the same themes as *La Guerre, yes sir!,* is nevertheless both less successful artistically and less significant than the earlier work. A major difference would seem to be that the struggle being described engages the loyalties of the author and the reader no more than it does those of Dorval's tenants.

Another obvious change lies in the author's portrayal of his characters and their lives; the affection infusing the treatment of the villagers has yielded here to a far more distanced and objective point of view.

Carrier's powers of poetic evocation of a time and place, of dreams and disappointments, are nowhere more fully realized than in *La Dame qui avait des chaînes aux chevilles (Lady with Chains)*, 1981. Virginie, who loves and marries Victor, then lives as a forest pioneer, knows the story of "The Lady," who had poisoned the innkeeper responsible for forcing her into a shameful existence, gone to prison, been released and sent to the New World where she had been able to build an honorable life. The book's structure, too artificially complex, presents at first alternating segments of "The Lady"'s story and Virginie's. The latter's plan to poison Victor begins in medias res and requires long flashbacks designed to create suspense as they build toward the pivotal scene in which, numbed and bewildered by a blizzard, Victor inadvertently leaves their baby to die. Pardoned in the end by the Church and by the court (both of which are shown in villainous light), the couple will share a new life, symbolized by the child in Virginie's womb.

Despite its contrived structure, a weak plot in which events seem to occur only because of authorial dictates rather than any necessity deriving either from characters or from circumstances, and a central figure whose motivations never become quite believable, *La Dame qui avait des chaînes aux chevilles* has impressive qualities. Carrier creates memorable personages both in the vignette presentation of "The Lady" and, especially, in Victor whose efforts to carve out a living from the wilderness strikingly evoke pioneer struggles. His monologues during the months of Virginie's silence express his optimism, his faith in life, and his great love in words of purest poetry.

Victor-Lévy Beaulieu (1945–   )

Victory-Lévy Beaulieu's increasingly vast literary production centers around a single fundamental problematics, that of the fiction-making process itself. His richly varied characters, many of whom reappear in book after book, exist and act as word structures of multilayered palimpsests in which present and past realities, memories, and dreams intermingle inextricably with imaginary beings, events, and resolutions. Thus we find that Abel Beauchemin, Beaulieu's fictionalized (and therefore distanced) double, has written all Beaulieu's novels and is in the process of writing all those that Beaulieu is announcing in advance. The degree of difference between the real and fictional authors is sometimes nonexistent, at others rather large; indeed, the process becomes even more convoluted as Beauchemin recognizes the extent to which all the characters *he* has created are in some ways merely portrayals of aspects of himself.

The entire Beaulieu canon can be read as a kind of purging of the writer's inner angst, a fleeing from solitude, self-indulgent in that it gives uninhibited rein to his fantasy and his need for invention, necessary as a form of autoanalysis whereby he might make it possible to go on living.

Among the novels considered in this study (as well as in others not included), Abel the writer is at the center of *Don Quichotte de la démanche* (*Don Quixote in Nighttown*), 1974, (narrated in the third person) and of *Monsieur Melville*, (*Monsieur Melville*), 1978, (in the first person). Though *Jos Connaissant* (*Jos Connaissant*), 1970, recounts the story of Abel's older brother, Abel is nonetheless one of the principal characters. Malcolm Hudd of *La Nuitte de Malcolm Hudd* (The night of Malcolm Hudd), 1969, is Jos's best friend, and an acquaintance of Abel. Milien Bérubé, protagonist of *Les Grands-Pères* (*The Grandfathers*), 1971, is Abel's maternal grandfather. Only Barthélémy Dupuis, the insane antihero of *Un Rêve québécois* (*A Québécois Dream*), 1972, appears not to belong to the immediate circle of the Beauchemin family, and yet he too makes reference to Malcolm and knows Fred, a policeman who is also known to Abel.

Since these texts exist as a kind of Chinese box of fictions, a potentially infinite regression of imaginings imagined, it is often impossible to determine on what level of reality a given episode takes place. As a consequence, and especially when one book is compared with another, there are disparities and contradictions. These differences, however, serve to emphasize the mythopoeic process as the subject that most concerns Beaulieu, for all exterior realities are inevitably subsumed into raw materials for creativity. Furthermore, the author's preoccupation with the act of writing leads him to essay numerous and varied experimental techniques. *La Nuitte de Malcolm Hudd* eschews the conventions of punctuation and capitalization, uses nonfunctional spelling deformations and runs words together for no apparent reason, employs parentheses idiosyncratically, and, before it ends, becomes its own metatext and self-critique, analyzing its author (and here the "I" seems intended to be Beaulieu himself), his sexuality, his anxieties, and the manner in which the various characters reflect his unconscious. Finally, emphasizing the unending nature of the imagination, the novel's end repeats its beginning.

Un Rêve québécois explores further techniques familiar to all readers of the French "New Novel," showing especially close affinities with the works of Alain Robbe-Grillet (and thus also with those of Hubert Aquin) in its deliberate sabotage of any possible reconstruction of the "reality" of situations, as opposed to Barthélémy's multiple (and mad) imaginings of them, as well as in its core of sexual obsession, sadism, murder, and mutilation.

Beaulieu's fascination with writing encompasses a deep-seated interest in other writers. He has published essays on several of them and book-length studies devoted to Victor Hugo and Jack Kerouac. His *Monsieur Melville,* which appeared in three separate volumes, is generally considered one of his most important works. In it, Beaulieu pursues his technical experimentation by deftly mingling fiction and reality and by defying all traditions of discrete boundaries between genres. On one level it is the autobiography of Beaulieu's reading and study of Herman Melville, presented as the account of Abel Beauchemin's identical actions. On another, it is a biography of Melville, with commentary by Beauchemin noting the many points of resemblance between himself and the American author. On still another level, Beaulieu has written a criticism and appreciation of Melville's entire corpus, marking in particular the increasing importance of poetry in Melville's final twenty-eight years. And, not least, the work is a fiction in which Beauchemin, aided by the protective love of the Indian girl Samm, becomes involved with Melville, writes part of his study of Melville in the nineteenth-century author's own home, retraces parts of Melville's travels, and having ultimately completed his reading and analysis, persuades Melville to leave the quays of New York and journey with him and Samm to Mattavinie. There they are greeted by Abel's father and several other characters from Beaulieu's fictions; and the long-promised writings of *La Grande Tribu* ("The Great Tribe," the opening part of "The True Saga of the Beauchemins") can now begin.

The autobiographical element in Beaulieu's work is obviously quite strong, and there is far more profundity than the surface interest in technique might indicate. His awareness of Quebec's political situtation comes repeatedly to the fore, for instance. Throughout the canon, the reader discovers the novelist's love and sorrow for the invisible country, this "suburb of America," ignored by its neighbors, with a literature that he excoriates for its lack of mythology, creativity, and life. He sees Quebec as a country that lacks the grandeur even of tragedy, an ambiguous land that both rejects and accepts Americanization.

The degree of Beaulieu's pessimism has diminished somewhat through the years. At no point was it greater than when he wrote *Un Rêve québécois*, which takes as its setting the virtual state of seige in North Montreal during the events of October, 1970, after a small group of separatist extremists had kidnapped a British commercial representative, then kidnapped and murdered the Quebec minister of labor. The very title of the novel demands a political reading, as do the names of the principal characters. Barthélémy represents a Quebecer Everyman, and the violence pervading all his actions, whether real or imagined, are efforts at liberation from the constant humiliations in his quotidian existence. His link with his French past (his wife, Jeanne d'Arc = Joan of Arc) is sterile (there is a stillborn child, a theme that recurs in *Don Quichotte de la démanche*); moreover, she betrays him with two persons whom he considers to be among his closest friends, Baptiste (the Church), and the policeman, Fred (the state, as well as the English in general). According to Beaulieu's analysis on the cover of the 1977 reprint of the novel, Lémy's violence againt Jeanne symbolizes an attempt at purification, a strange aspiration toward holiness, toward control of his own reality. Yet, though Lémy speaks of the two-hundred-year-old rebellion and envisions a hundred thousand replicas of himself marching triumphantly to a future, Beaulieu puts little faith in this madman's reverie. From beginning to end the police have the upper hand; Lémy perpetrates his violence seemingly only in a kind of psychodrama that may be personally cathartic but that destroys nothing but his own home; that is, his dream, as Beaulieu presents it, in no wise affects any other external reality.

In spite of passages that offer no indulgence whatever for what Beaulieu continues to perceive as Quebec's weaknesses, the positive side of his attitude comes through more clearly in recent works. Don Quichotte exclaims to Abel that the very word "Québécois" evokes the ideas of "likable" and "vast." And as Beauchemin plans the writing of his *La Grande Tribu*, he sees himself both as a citizen of his country, the "country of sources," and as a writer somehow allied with great, tranquil forces that exceed national boundaries. Additionally, full account must be taken of one of the major thematics of Beaulieu's works, that of "possibilities," a notion that often occurs in juxtaposition with mentions of Quebec. His unwillingness to tolerate adherence to any but the highest standards admits, nevertheless, occasional glimmers of optimism for Quebec's future.

Similarly, his effort to be able to talk about his people (a necessary corollary of his hopes to be able to speak of himself) is evolving into one of Quebec's most significant literary monuments. One might wish that Beaulieu had been less tolerant of some of his excesses, that he had yielded less often to glib solutions, that he had chosen to edit more judiciously. Yet even this failing has its compensations, for rarely has a writer revealed himself so thoroughly to the reader, not merely in his weaknesses, but also in what emerges as a humbly vulnerable goodness, gentleness, and loving nature.

His works are not meant, however, as a memorial to himself—that they allow us to know the writer so well is but a fortuitous result of the honesty of his manner. Rather they are a homage to a moment in history, a way of life seized in all its transitory beauty, neither idealized nor denigrated. The Beauchemin clan forms the nucleus, but a whole world of dreams, ambitions, sufferings, disappointments, triumphs, loneliness, and love revolves around them, first in their native village, then in the underprivileged (i.e., francophone) areas of North Montreal. The impact of urbanization on individuals remains one of the dominant themes of Quebec's writers. Paradoxically, there is perhaps not a single work among those Beaulieu has published so far that could qualify outrightly as a masterpiece. But the value of the whole greatly surpasses that of the separate parts. It is only as the reader enters further into the writer's intimacy, as the extravagances of one book are corrected by the truths of another, that it becomes possible to appreciate the epic sweep of what is developing into a true saga.

Suzanne Paradis (1936–   )

Suzanne Paradis, whose work has been woefully neglected by critics, is undeniably one of the finest of Quebec's contemporary poets and novelists. To downplay her novels as facile and redundant or repetitious reveals a serious shortsightedness; in fact, Paradis's writing talents are prodigious but controlled. Moreover, her novels must be read as an organic whole, works building one upon the other, illuminating one another's characters, and demanding intense concentration if readers are to comprehend a tortuous world in which fear and chaos intermingle with happiness and peace, and banal, demonstrable reality conflicts with other realities, nebulous, marvelous, fantastic. One might refer to Paradis's book of literary criticism, *Femme fictive, femme réelle: le personnage féminin dans le roman féminin canadien-français* (Fictional woman, real woman: female characters in French-Canadian feminine novels), 1966 and aptly describe her own heroines as at once fictitious and real, belonging to and thriving in worlds of novelistic verisimilitude and of cosmic enchantment. They are, simultaneously or alternatively, one and doubles. Further, as with Anne Hébert, whose prose shows strong traces of her poetic writings, Paradis's style is highly poeticized, although considerably more fluid than Hébert's staccato phrasings.

The female protagonists in works such as *Emmanuelle en noir* (Emmanuelle in black), 1971, and *Un Portrait de Jeanne Joron* (A portrait of Jeanne Joron), 1977 (or, for that matter, *Les Cormorans* [The cormorants], 1968; *Quand la terre était toujours jeune* ["When the Earth Was Still Young"], 1974; *L'Eté sera chaud* [A hot summer in store], 1975), are essentially rebellious figures refusing not only their personal lot in life as beings relegated by society to a marginal existence but also the unacceptable absurdity of orthodox, absolutist sociomoral value systems. Mired in a stultifying conventional universe, Paradis's heroines assert their fundamental need for freedom, certainly one of the major themes in the author's entire canon. Drawn by sympathetic magic into mysterious, visionary other worlds, Emmanuelle in *Emmanuelle en noir* and Amélie in *Un Portrait de Jeanne Joron* thereby realize their profoundest authentic selves and give reality to what might otherwise remain mere signs and symbols of freedom. But these characters are, at the same time, a prey to torments and doubts stemming from the society in which they must somehow function (or make excuses for apparently doing so), as well as from tumultuous inner tensions and passions. In Paradis's novels destiny and fatality appear to form necessary elements of revolt and liberty— her female characters come to know variants of ineluctable doom, for the obverse of their strength is helplessness, the complement to their sense of unity is disquieting instability, the end result of their quest for total open expression of self is judgment and condemnation. Each is in some way a victim of narrow, negative institutionalized norms which assign her ultimate fate: in *Emmanuelle en noir* Emmanuelle's madness is considered to be as morally validated as is Amélie's commitment to a psychiatric home in *Un Portrait de Jeanne Joron;* in *Miss Charlie* (Miss Charlie), 1979, the eponymous heroine's panicked, desperate attempts at self-possession of her true identity lead to schizoid irreconcilability. While Paradis's protagonists lay claim to the right to their authenticity and their powers and beliefs, destiny seems to proclaim a manner of defeat, or absence, or death.

In ways again reminiscent of Hébert, in all three novels under study here Paradis explores the interplay between reality and appearances, the various coalescing depth and surface structures of the books' narratives, and the doubling psyches of their principal characters. For the author, the outward, tangible, social, cultural, and moral (and, in Miss Charlie's case, artistic) milieu in which her female figures exist comprises no more than an illusory effect of that existence, a pretext to which society requires strict adherence. Beyond this superficial deceit (that is, a given realistic situational context) lie higher planes and dimensions of the characters' true and total self and world. In *Un Portrait de Jeanne Joron* Jeanne and her father, Lascot, lead Amélie to "see" the vast possibilities within the depths of the human psyche, where global vision takes its roots, to perceive "presences" beyond the impoverished limits of the mortal gaze. In *Miss Charlie* the writer Gordon Mortimer brings Marie-Charles Craig (Miss Charlie) to seek and discover "other" and different components of her physical life and psychological self, less readily communicated, less easily accepted also. "To see other presences": the expression could appropriately serve as an epigraph to Paradis's novels and poetry in their entirety; the words form primordial elements of her privileged lexicon.

"Harmony" is another recurring term and notion in her books, for her female characters (and the male figure of Lascot) seek a state of harmony that would void any Manichaean view of the universe and in which opposing forces and opposite values would meld through a process of communicative silence and solitude. That process is perhaps best exemplified by Jeanne and Lascot, in a visionary mode, and sociopsychologically by Miss Charlie in the act of writing, that is, of telling herself, inventing herself. For them, and likewise for Emmanuelle and Amélie, the final aim is the discovery of the self's limitlessness of being, and the revelation and actual experience of that truth. In this perspective Emmanuelle's madness is not to be interpreted in the ordinary judgmental acceptation of the phenomenon; Miss Charlie's fear and confusion are apparent only: it is her fecund imagination that holds sway; *Un Portrait de Jeanne Joron* comes to a close with a lengthy quasi-documentary statement of Amélie's old age and implied death—until the reader reaches the narrator's very last words which disavow Amélie's death as event, and shift (once and for all?) the novel's dual themes of mortality and immortality toward the latter.

Whether, in *Emmanuelle en noir*, examining and giving full credence to unknown regions of the psyche generally feared and repulsed by Western communal moral systems, or presenting as fact an interplanetary vision of existent other worlds in *Un Portrait de Jeanne Joron*, or asserting, in *Miss Charlie*, the due place in life of mental, psychological, and artistic fantasy, mystery, and what one might call unabashedly and overtly eccentric manifestations, Paradis strikes out against the obtuse bumptiousness of prevailing human knowledge and norms of behavior acceptance. In *Miss Charlie*, however, she develops the multiplex forms of writing itself far more considerably than in her previous novels. *Un Portrait de Jeanne Joron*, for instance, articulates Amélie's split personality and metamorphosing cosmos by relatively conventional, though nonetheless remarkable cross-shiftings of characteral and narratorial identities, "I" and "Amélie." *Miss Charlie*, on the other hand, contains three principal narrative levels and modes (and possible additional ancillary ones), telescoping one into the other, antiphonal in the responsive alternations of their narrational voices. Yet at the same time each possesses its own autonomy in the psychological particulars of its characters and the unique writing creativity of its authors, and by specific type fonts—roman, italic, boldface. Miss Charlie is the plausible (rather than any demonstrably true) chronicler of the surface narrative, a matter-of-fact account of Marie-Charles's daily existence. Threatened and challenged by the (imaginary?) concoctions of a new neighbor, novelist Gordon Mortimer, Miss Charlie becomes a fabulist in her own right, inventing the work's second-level narrative. The third narrative level consists of Marie-Charles's translation of *The Snowman*, the novel ostensibly authored by Mortimer which he is about to finish. Moreover, characteral identities change nominally from one narrative to another (Chinchilla and Charlie, e.g.) or assume different genders (female Charlie, and male Charlie Blackburn in *The Snowman,* e.g.).

The point to recall is that Paradis, with spectacular mastery of her creative poetic and descriptive narrative gifts, puts forth in *Miss Charlie* themes and vision-beliefs that have been integral parts of all her prose writings to date. The major female "presences" (in Paradisian terminology) in *Emmanuelle en noir* and *Un Portrait de Jeanne Joron* reflect the presence/absence syndrome of the polyvalent lives that they lead, the ecstasy of discovery of all that is socially unsanctioned "other," the pallor of expected moral life-routine. *Miss Charlie's* variant-level characters, its open-ended bimodal fiction/reality may possess distinctive traits and special configurations, but for Paradis all compose, in fact, emanations from, extensions of a multitude of selves and realms of experience contained within a unique self: This and Other, Here and Elsewhere, Within and Without, Past, Present, and Future, Life and Death. Paradisian characters are at once personae and, in the Jungian sense, persona and anima, simultaneously: fictional presentations and real beings reflecting the game roles that they are conditioned to play in life while also incarnating archetypal global, cosmic ideals to which they are accorded preternatural access.

As a novelist, Paradis aims to reveal the threadbare substance of notions of destiny and morality that conventional wisdom construes as inviolable, and no less to expose the shabby limitations of received material appearances and spiritual concepts traditionally viewed as vehicles of sole and unique truth. Accordingly, readers should attune themselves to the author's expansive and illuminating mythos of experiential multivalence in overlapping realms of the individual's mundane entity and imponderable imaginability.[1]

Louky Bersianik (1930–   )

As a polemicist and satirist, Louky Bersianik (pseudonym of Lucille Durand) easily invites comparison with the world's greatest practitioners of those genres. In her writings, all totally committed to the struggle for women's rights, fiction becomes only one of many techniques useful for illustrating the points she makes. Plot is virtually nonexistent; characters, little more than names attached to recognizable views and attitudes, sometimes reappear from one novel to the other. When fiction does occur as more than the merest veneer, it is in the form of sharp, telling anecdotes, often cast as pastiches or as parables, some transparent, others hauntingly enigmatic.

L'Euguélionne (The Euguélionne), 1976, called by its author a triptych novel, employs a slim science-fiction device as an introduction to its contents. The Euguélionne, a super-intelligent Everywoman figure, arrives on earth from some distant planet as she carries on her quest for her "positive planet" and the male of her species. At the end of the work she decides that this planet offers no answer and she leaves in order to pursue her search elsewhere. In the interim she meets and hears the stories of many people and, moreover, examines vast numbers of the world's books. The primary message of the triptych consists of what might be perceived as a running debate with Sigmund Freud ("St. Siegfried") and Jacques Lacan ("Jacques Linguant") and psychology, psychoanalysis, and psychiatry in general with regard to their theories concerning women. Freud's ideas on penis-envy and some of Lacan's pronouncements on the phallus are special objects of the author's attacks. Bersianik wins the debate hands down, effectively deriding and counterbalancing those theories. The work is not, however, limited to these issues. It comprises, rather, a summum that touches at greater or lesser length on virtually every issue of interest to feminists. Bersianik usually maintains a substantial degree of objectivity, and for the most part she carefully thinks through her arguments, studying all sides of most complex questions, only rarely taking a dogmatic stance. Even when the reader may disagree with her ideas or conclusions, the intelligence of her presentation remains admirable.

The goals, concepts, and basic techniques of *Le Pique-nique sur l'Acropole* (Picnic on the Acropolis), 1979, are largely akin to those of *L'Euguélionne.* A parody of Plato's *Symposium,* the work consists of discussions, not of love per se, but of female sexuality. Socrates is linked to Freud and Lacan as a promulgator of particularly odious and ludicrous notions, and finally Xanthippe gets to express her side of the story of their marriage. Bersianik feels strongly and makes the reader feel strongly about the fate of women in the twenty-six countries where clitoridectomy and infibulation are still commonly practiced. The emphasis on the factual is underlined by copious footnotes and even the inclusion of a bibliograpahy. Less ambitious than *L'Euguélionne, Le Pique-nique sur l'Acropole* nevertheless succeeds remarkably in achieving what it attempts. As a satire of the *Sym-*

posium, it is very funny; as a discussion of the sexuality of women, it is disturbing when it means to be, seemingly thorough, and often quite moving.

In general, Bersianik's techniques are more commonly associated with the essay than with fiction—a deliberate choice growing out of the nature of her material and in no way indicating limitations on her talent. Dialogue, for instance, sometimes bears little or no resemblance to actual conversation, but often consists of monologues, storytelling, speech-making, or rather artificial, stilted exchanges in which the message is far more important than the medium and by which there is virtually no differentiation of characters. And yet the author is fully capable, when she so desires, of writing that reflects all the individuality and spontaneity of everyday discourse; by interspersing these lighter, more properly novelistic passages at intervals throughout her work, she adds greatly to its readability and popular appeal. Further adding to this readability in *L'Euguélionne* are the work's inner divisions. While the three "panels" represent no more than stages in the Euguélionne's visit to this planet (which may be summarized as: 1. Arrival; 2. Information-gathering; 3. The Euguélionne's message to the world, followed by her departure), the panels themselves are subdivided respectively into 25, 90, and 97 numbered parts, usually indicating a shift in either subject, point of view, or rhetorical technique. The Rabelaisian exuberance (Bersianik makes several specific references to Rabelais), energy, and all-inclusiveness with which the author musters her arguments and materials, coupled with the diversity and wit of her descriptions, command the reader's attention. But though her ideas are often laced with playfulness, their "substantive marrow" remains the central concern, and Bersianik's methods are so varied as to include overtly didactic and hortatory passages.

The series of speeches in *Le Pique-nique sur l'Acropole* is, of course, a direct reflection of the model being pastiched, but Bersianik had already demonstrated in *L'Euguélionne* that such a pattern was quite compatible with her own talent. Indeed, by far the largest part of the earlier work, including most of the dialogues, is recounted by the Euguélionne—i.e., Bersianik's technique is to give a predominantly first-person account narrated by a personage seen from the outside. The distancing thus achieved increases, rather than diminishes, the authority of the ideas expressed, for the Euguélionne represents greater wisdom and experience than any ordinary human could claim. Like Montesquieu's pseudo-Persians, this "outsider" quite naturally sees situations in fresh and interesting ways, balances them against a different set of values, and judges them accordingly. But Bersianik, unlike Montesquieu, never lets her characters play the role of the naive innocent; the Euguélionne does not so much wonder as condemn the oppressors and sympathize with the oppressed, while at the same time suggesting and encouraging profound social change. Moreover, since the attitudes and practices denounced herein exist throughout the world, only an extraterrestrial can pretend to an objective point of view; Bersianik's chosen polemical method thus necessitates recourse to science fiction.

In like manner, *Le Pique-nique sur l'Acropole* ignores the irrelevancies of the realistic, naturalistic tradition in favor of abolition of normal boundaries of time and space, for the ultimate object of attack, namely, the inequities forced upon women, have never known any such limits. And just as the Euguélionne represents superhuman qualities of a type associated with divinity, so too does *Le Pique-nique sur l'Acropole* achieve mythological dimensions when, at the end, Avertine brings one of the caryatids of the Erechtheum to life, liberating her thus from her millenia-old bondage, then goes to sleep in her arms.

Gilbert La Rocque (1943–1984)

Recounted by Serge, as both character and, a not uncommon literary device, omniscient author, Gilbert La Rocque's *Serge d'entre les morts* (Serge from among the dead), 1976, records the protagonist's efforts, recognized as doomed to failure, to exorcise his haunted memories of childhood and adolescence. The reader reconstructs the chronological sequence of events, starting with the courting of Serge's grandmother, Aurore, and ending with the present of the actual narration of those events, far removed in time and space from Serge's youthful years in the house his grandfather, Piphane, and his sons built for the family. The narrator, however, is not concerned with the linear progression of happenings, but rather with the ever-recurring phantasms of death, sex, and longed-for liberation which overrun his consciousness.

The novel is, in part, the tale of the central character's sexual awakening, of his frustrated desire for his cousin Colette, who is also his stepsister, of his earliest awkward carnal experiences up to the moment at which he becomes reasonably self-assured, and of the perpetuation of his obsession for Colette. This tale of an erotic possession unfolds against a backdrop engulfed by the odors of rot and decay. Serge's thoughts return incessantly to memories of the night on which his father died, primarily recalled in terms of his impressions as a five-year-old child; to the death of Colette's mother, as experienced by her husband; and, above all, to the interminable agony, the living death of the senile grandmother, her family unsure of the extent to which she might still understand as she lives out her life in the room that she entered permanently, nailing down the window shades, after Piphane's death. As realized (or imagined) by Serge, the grandmother's recollections and reactions occupy a large portion of the book, just as the creak of her constant rocking, her chosen method of fending off the encroaching ghosts of her own dead, pervades the entire house, which Serge perceives as a vast extension of Aurore.

For Serge these many losses represent parts of a never-ending cycle of wasted lives and shattered dreams, yielding an eternal and monstrous despair. The notion of rigidity, of imprisonment in encapsulated ahistory, of the virtual impossibility of meaningful change, dominates much of the character's psyche. As he matures, these are the bonds from which he must break free. Following Aurore's death, he tries to erase the memory of her presence by an attempted seduction in her room, and later, by casting out her gold teeth (symbol of an overly powerful permanence), and ransacking all her carefully preserved clothing and personal effects. He pulses with the incendiary urge to destroy the house utterly; it is an act that he aborts, and, instead, his departure from the house replaces its destruction. Years later, as La Rocque's protagonist ends his confessional account of these obsessions, he comes to realize that the circle of perpetual rebeginnings cannot be broken, that his personal demons will be with and within him forever.

The grim and grotesque novelistic universe of *Les Masques* (The masks), 1980, presents a corrosive vision of the world and too many of its beings; despite the symbolism of potential hope and renascence (the closing dawn sequence, specifically), it cannot avoid or alleviate a pervasively crushing pessimism. Death is one of the most obsessional themes in La Rocque's novels, but of far greater significance are the interrelated themes of separation and survival. Alain, *Les Masques*'s protagonist, both as child-I and adult-He, attempts throughout the book to understand and come to terms with rejection(s), with the love and hate that rejection inevitably causes. His mother's premature death from cancer is felt primarily as an abandonment of the child, who similarly nurtures a bitter resentment against his father for the latter's refusal to keep him, turning him over, instead, to sundry relatives and like a coward fleeing in the night. Alain's wife, Anne, lost in her neuroses, leaves him inexplicably, another separation and an especially painful one for Alain's survival. The lengthiest (recurring) sequence of *Les Masques* recounts the single most devastating separation: the accidental drowning of Alain's young son during the daylong birthday party for Alain's grandfather. Yet here again the anguish, loneliness, and despair are occasioned not so much by death itself as by Alain's having rejected his son just prior to the accident. And was it, indeed, an accident?—for the book points transparently to the son's hurt, his quiet determination to react to his father's physical scolding, the father's shame at having irrationally struck the child in public. The narrator-character's guilt and rage, his disgust, repugnance, and loathing of all humanity stem from his sense of helplessness faced with the fact of separation, the need for survival. Clearly at the heart of La Rocque's works is his protagonists' difficulty in accepting the responsibility for what is deemed to be an irresponsibility—either their own or that of others.

La Rocque is a remarkable master of multiple-sense imagery (visual, tactile, olfactory), making the first chapter's restaurant scene a probing insight into the creative process—faked memory sliding into true novel-fact, author metamorphosing imperceptibly into narrator, narrator into character, back to author overviewing his work as it is being written—and a vicious, sarcastically funny satire of certain types among the critical establishment, under the circumstances, Véronique Flibotte, book reviewer for *La Gazelle*. The entire drowning episode, adumbrated in the first chapter and fully developed in the third (and last), is a gripping experience that the reader lives that much more closely as author-narrator-character have now coalesced into first-person "I" or a parenthetically interpolated "he-I." Child and adult, Eric and Alain, past and present, flow back and forth, looping the loop of the book's characterial and situational components, manifestly spanning a thirty-year period in one individual life but exploding into a drama of vaster proportion:

the permanence of failure and solitude in the irreversible cycle of eternity and absurdity.

Gilbert La Rocque was one of the most gifted of Quebec's contemporary novelists (and dramatists), and as literary director of the Québec/Amérique publishing house he was one of the major forces in the promulgation of the novel. His untimely death at the age of forty-one will be keenly felt as a loss to Quebec's total literary history.

Yves Beauchemin (1941–   )

Le Matou (The Tomcat), 1981, is Yves Beauchemin's genial second novel; an immediate best-seller in Canada and France, it represents a milestone in the history of the Quebec novel. On the surface it is a fast-paced adventure yarn, sometimes harrowing, often very funny, pitting the "good guys" against the "bad guys," with the former seeming to win, though not without having to put up a virtually superhuman struggle. It is to the author's credit that he is able, through his acute observational talent and master storytelling gifts, to capture the reader's attention and to keep it riveted for the whole of a near-600-page book.

As meritorious as it is on that level, however, *Le Matou,* on deeper planes, develops more significant allegorical tales. Taking his cues from the rich legacy of the novel of quest, Beauchemin presents his principal character, Florent, in search of personal liberty and self-sufficiency in a society dominated by power and greed. Subversively demolishing that novelistic lineage, the author has his protagonist resort to the very means and tools of oppression against which he rebels, and in so doing he assures his ultimate failure to free himself from the malevolent forces of destiny, a destiny that is a carnivorous form of terror named Egon Ratablavasky. One of the most fascinating and frightening creations of modern fiction, Ratablavasky, omnipresent and omniscient, symbolizes the strength and evil of money in a merciless capitalistic society. He is the ruling master class that, for reasons of fancy or whimsy, chooses its victims and crushes them, or elects its successors—provided they are capable of enduring grueling and mystifying initiation rites and rituals. Florent's millionairess aunt at times appears to be an eerie accomplice of Ratablavasky's in inflicting punishment or offering recompense to Florent in his attempts to be proprietor of his restaurant, that is, in the book's conceptual scheme, to be his own person.

In the picaresque manner *Le Matou*'s fabric consists of certain threads woven to their necessary ends, within the confines of the novel's universe, but with numerous other strands left untied. Hence Captain Galarneau's mysterious suggestion that the fearsome financier Egon Ratablavasky is not the tyrannical "outsider" to francophone Quebec society, but Ernest Robichaud, Quebecer through and through. Florent's aunt is a displaced Quebecer, having betrayed herself to the moneyed oppressor to the South; the noted French chef Aurélien Picquot vituperates against America's domination and destruction (albeit of quick food and haute cuisine respectively— but humor is the book's guise); the "damned anglophone" Slipskin is both Ratablavasky's associate and victim. The text thus validates sociopolitical readings inherent in the whole of French-speaking Canada's literary tradition.

A sense of fatalism pervades *Le Matou,* incarnated by Ratablavasky and the child "Mister Emile." Not even the vicious revenge inflicted by Mister Emile's cat, Breakfast, can destroy the evil of the old "stranger" and release Florent from his grip; and Ratablavasky goes on to brutally provoke the child's death. Beauchemin thus structures his dual theme: both loss of autonomy and loss of innocence are permanent and irrevocable in specific human natures and in the evolution of humanity. The significance of *Le Matou* does not reside in the psychological analysis of its characters, which is, in fact, facile and shallow, nor in any radically innovative facet of novelistic endeavors. Going beyond its humor and local color, the novel plumbs the reality of a pitiless world in which happiness must always be a somewhat sullied affair, successful self-realization a faulty mechanism, society an enemy of which one can at best be helplessly chary. Beauchemin's novel symbolizes, by its characters and situations, the overwhelming moral turpitude of what has come to be known as twentieth-century man. The sole remaining possible solace emanates from friendship, in the most fundamental sense of that fact, and in its principal, though double-edged ally, memory: as the corrective for future hope, as the remembrance of past suffering. Beauchemin weaves a surface plot of incredible adventures, false trails, unexpected reversals and encounters, all colored by a cruel irony. Using forms and techniques liberally borrowed from baroque and detective novels, the author lends to his book a constant ambience of mystery and suspense. Numerous characters appear in this vast North American fresco; certain of them are brief sketches only, while others are more carefully delineated in a story that often wanders into the fantastic. Beauchemin punctuates a precise sort of realism with sudden violent eruptions and fantasy sequences that give the novel a hostile and uneasy atmosphere. The universe that the author depicts is exposed to subversive, vaguely comprehensible threats to the desires and hopes of individuals confronted by an all-consuming evil.

Le Matou's realism only serves to unmask the inevitable terror that roams below comforting external appearances. Florent and his friend Picquot are paralyzed, their innocence and goodness whittled down under the nefarious influence of Ratablavasky and his baleful accomplice, Captain Galarneau. The diabolic knight of a civilization bent on annihilating itself, Ratablavasky unleashes the fury of the rich against the poor; money, in Beauchemin's view, can take every liberty, and first and foremost that of destroying liberty itself, considered a cumbersome commodity once it no longer is the prerogative of the superior race. Money equals evil, evil equals exploitation, exploitation equals oppression, suppression, death. Cupidity and aggressivity afflict Ratablavasky and aunt Jeunehomme to the point that neither one is able to or wants to curb this need for power and will.

In a largely destructive world Florent (as opposed to Elise, his wife, and Picquot, both of whom are from the outset somewhat more lucid, less blinded by illusions) travels the road from innocence and naiveté to cynicism and disillusionment. On the other hand, Mister Emile's total pessimism veers toward a glimmer of optimism, but then the tragedy of death strikes. These two characters, at least, reveal a certain level of awareness that might perhaps even be akin to a spiritual quest; the end effect in each case, however, is a signal failure occasioned by a society that the author stigmatizes as morally deficient, indeed irresponsible. The death of Florent's soul is but the inadmissible counterpart to Mister Emile's physical death. Florent is ultimately forced to admit that knowledge of self brings neither inner peace nor any equitable sharing of the public weal.

Le Matou's distorted fantasy world, nonetheless, spreads forth a whole network of realistic imprints, the most obvious of which is the fact of daily work, a fact that, in Western society, is assumed to guarantee secure social adaptation, a solid moral sense, the realization of dreams and hopes. In truth, the novel underscores the debasement that results from work, and the misery that the lack of work inflicts, once capitalistic society sets its monster in motion, that is, the persecution of the working classes. Beauchemin radically denounces this socioeconomic calamity, this form of alienation of the human being reduced to a state of absurd humiliation. Ratablavasky's money is his guarantor of personal freedom whereas Florent's destiny is subjection. The author refutes the sacral Western myth of work, and allows it not a redemptive function but a degrading intent that leads man to abject suffering rather than to his joyous liberation. In this perspective *Le Matou* unfolds as a series of Florent's crushing discoveries, which occur within a temporal and spatial framework peculiar to Beauchemin's vision. The author juxtaposes a pathetic, inward-looking Quebec, a United States that is insidious because of its insolent power and vulgar wealth, and a cosmos of mythical configurations; hence the ambivalence, in a long and complex book that does not readily demarcate fantasy-novel, ironic text, and sociomoral, politico-economic statement.

Beauchemin tells a tale of shared love and friendship, but one from which he excludes blatant traces of banal, pretentious romanticism. His themes are articulated on sequences of destruction and disquieting signs and symbols that are reminders or interventions of Ratablavasky's domination and the submission of his victims, and that underline the notions of persecuted innocence and the impossibility of happiness and accomplishment. Beneath the grotesque masks worn by events and objects that are motivated by a voluntaristic evil, a more hideous reality overwhelms the protagonists' lives: unemployment and poverty, hunger, cold, miscarriage, attempted poisoning—the horrors of anguish and desolation. Beauchemin, in final analysis, passes a somber sentence on the human condition, on man's efforts to combat the forces of darkness and to triumph over evil.

A retrospective glance on the events of past years in Quebec enlightens the reader on the enigmatic character of Ratablavasky. It is not by happenstance that Pierre Elliott Trudeau figures in *Le Matou*, among other things, in reference to his *Federalism and the French Canadians*, which Abbé Jeunehomme cavalierly treads under foot. Both Ratablavasky and Trudeau have authored texts, each adopts a falsely pious attitude'toward others, and each is obsessed by power and domination. Thus, by a caricatural distortion of char-

acter and fictional context, Beauchemin brings into question the
former prime minister and his sociopolitical vision of Canada and,
more specifically, of francophone Quebec's role and standing within
the country. This ideological resonance underlies the entire book
and thereby makes it a deadly satire of Canada's former Master.
Altogether loathsome, Ratablavasky is, on the novel's narrative level,
responsible for all the evils that befall Florent and Elise and, on the
larger level of novel as fable, for all the alienating evils that society
perpetrates on its citizens.

What is seen as in serious danger of crumbling is Quebecers'
socioeconomic and political power and, consequently, their cultural
life. Ratablavasky/Robichaud, strong in his arrogance and money,
thirsty for omnipotence, is not unlike the Trudeau bilingual monster. Like the Quebec politician, Ratablavasky promises freedom and
autonomy, the better to assure the anonymity of the earth's emas-
culated. Both the province and the individual are immorally enticed
into cradling fond hopes that are no more than idle illusions. As
soon as Florent seeks to exercise his individuality in all its plenitude,
as soon as Quebec rises too overtly in revolt against abuses of two
centuries' standing, the dream of possession becomes the nightmare
of dispossession. Florent's hopelessness squares with the province's
social collapse. Trudeau was no less a traitor figure during the
referendum campaign for Quebec's independence than Ratablavasky
is toward his middle-class ward. In either case, power and autonomy
are refused because both are judged components of a dangerous
sharing in a fundamentally hierarchical state. On one side, Florent
is signatory to a contract that bends him under the yoke of the
bilingual financier; on the other, Quebec is forced to accept a basically anglophone national constitution that rends asunder its so-
ciolinguistic unity.

Here and elsewhere, satire and parody impart to the work a special
tonality that creates a universe apart, a novelistic reality that often
remains unverifiable in its thematic recurrences. Beauchemin leads
the reader to the core of a brutal and Manichaean world in which
some form of death destroys feelings of goodness and beauty, and
which functions according to its own inner coherence and logic.
Although the reader recognizes a number of anguishing traits of
contemporary man, this astonishing work tends, all in all, toward
the allegory, the parable. *Le Matou* is a fable of the Master and the
Slave wherein Ratablavasky-Mephistopheles buys the soul of Florent-

Faust; ultimately, however, *Le Matou* evolves as Beauchemin's spectacle of the imagination faced with the indecipherable enigma of destiny.

Note

1. This study of Suzanne Paradis's novelistic output was limited to those works under consideration here strictly because, at the time of my writing, the author was in the process of revising her first six novels. While some of the works had only lexical and stylistic changes, others, such as *Un Portrait de Jeanne Joron,* underwent modification even at the narratorial and characterial levels. Forthcoming essays will deal in detail with the revised corpus.

Chapter Five
Conclusion

Prose writings in French Canada from the sixteenth through the eighteenth century were, with certain exceptions which are now being reevaluated for their literary qualities per se, mainly of a documentary nature, shedding light on the ethnology and demography of a land in the midst of colonization processes. These historical accounts, chronicles, and religious tracts, are revealing for an understanding of the times, as, indeed, an enormous journalistic output is for the nineteenth century. The latter century's novels, by and large, reveal a heavy-handed proselytism geared to theological preachings in social, cultural, and moral matters. Rare was the novelist who dared brave Church fanaticism and censorship by practicing writing as a free art form, independent of canonical formulae.

Although the religico-patriotic legacy endures into the twentieth century, the novel (and poetry and theater no less so) assumes more inflammatory polemical characteristics and wages frontal attacks on supposedly forbidden grounds: sexuality and politics, the inner individual as a profane and self-contained being, responsible and answerable to human-bound ethical principles. Writers seize upon free-rein imagination to explode sacrosanct Quebec social and cultural myths and to produce a new exploratory literature composed, often, of gratuitous game and dynamic commitment. Artist Paul-Emile Borduas's *Refus global* (1948), a manifesto compared to André Breton's Surrealist manifestos for its intransigently anticonformist stance, rallied artists, poets, and novelists in a call for total liberation in all domains. Its influence, as Breton's in France, ripples in the arts still today. Similarly, early awakenings of a national, or state, conscience have echoes of greater intensity in the formulation of the journal *Cité Libre* (Free city) in the 1950s, and more so within the folds of *Parti pris* in the mid-1960s. The latter brings to the forefront of Quebec letters Marxist literary criticism and (by usual seepage mechanism) artistic creation; it also propels a controversy over language that lingers into the 1980s. Rebelling against slavish imitation of France's colonizing language, *Parti pris* writers urge bold use of joual, postulated as a political lever for repossessing what these writers consider Quebec identity, as well as for repelling sociocultural suppression. This controversial linguistic attitude has, however, produced more detractors than adherents.

Perhaps the most striking aspect of the Quebec novel since the 1960s is its extraordinary ebullience and variety, its astonishing quantity and quality. Within properly literary forms, certain novelists incline toward sociological or political orientations (e.g., Godbout and Aquin), historico-mythological concoctions (e.g., Ferron), poetic prose grafted onto recognizable, tangible realities (e.g., Hébert, Paradis, and Maheux-Forcier), enterprises of epic proportions (e.g., Victor-Lévy Beaulieu), fantasy fables (e.g., Carrier), parody/paradox/caricature (e.g., Beauchemin and Bessette), genial wordplay in parables of childhood and adolescence (e.g., Ducharme), visionary worlds of utopian male/female social restructuration (e.g., Bersianik).

It is this commitment to a language and a geography, a culture and a society that happen to be francophone on an anglophone North American continent that assures an eminent future to Quebec letters. It is this resounding eclecticism that promises continued artistic creativity of the highest order from established novelists and talented neophytes alike.

Selected Bibliography

PRIMARY SOURCES

Authors are listed alphabetically; works of each author are listed chronologically by date of publication.

Angers, Félicité. See Conan, Laure.

Aquin, Hubert. *Prochain épisode.* Montréal: Le Cercle du Livre de France, 1965. *Prochain épisode.* Translated by Penny Williams. Toronto: McClelland & Stewart, 1973.

————. *Trou de mémoire.* Montréal: Le Cercle du Livre de France, 1968. *Blackout.* Translated by Alan Brown. Toronto: House of Anansi, 1974.

————. *L'Antiphonaire.* Montréal: Le Cercle du Livre de France, 1969. *The Antiphonary.* Translated by Alan Brown. Toronto: House of Anansi, 1973.

Aubert de Gaspé, Philippe. *Les Anciens Canadiens.* Québec: Desbarats et Derbishire, 1863. First appeared in *Les Soirées canadiennes,* 1862; a revised, corrected version of 1864 forms the basis for the 1961 Fides edition, Montréal. *Canadians of Old.* Translated by Charles Roberts. Toronto: McClelland & Stewart, 1974.

Baillargeon, Pierre. *Les Médisances de Claude Perrin.* Montréal: Editions Parizeau, 1945. (The cynicism of Claude Perrin)

————. *Commerce.* Montréal: Editions Variétés, 1947. (Commerce)

Beauchemin, Yves. *Le Matou.* Montréal: Editions Québec/Amérique, 1981. *The Tomcat.* Translated by Sheila Fischman. Toronto: McClelland & Stewart, 1986.

Beaulieu, Victor-Lévy. *La Nuitte de Malcolm Hudd.* Montréal: Editions du Jour, 1969. (The night of Malcolm Hudd)

————. *Jos Connaissant.* Montréal: Editions du Jour, 1970. *Jos Connaissant.* Translated by Raymond Chamberlain. Toronto: Exile Editions, 1982.

————. *Les Grands-Pères.* Montréal: Editions du Jour, 1971. *The Grandfathers.* Translated by Marc Plourde. Montreal: Harvest House, 1975.

————. *Un Rêve québécois.* Montréal: Editions du Jour, 1972. *A Québécois Dream.* Translated by Raymond Chamberlain. Toronto: Exile Editions, 1978.

————. *Don Quichotte de la Démanche.* Montréal: Editions de L'Aurore, 1974. *Don Quixote in Nighttown.* Translated by Sheila Fischman. Victoria: Press Porcépic, 1978.

————. *Monsieur Melville.* Vol. 1: *Dans les aveilles de Moby Dick;* Vol. 2: *Lorsque souffle Moby Dick;* Vol. 3: *L'Après Moby Dick ou la souveraine poésie.* Montréal: VLB Editeur, 1978. *Monsieur Melville.* Vol. 1: *On the Eve of Moby Dick;* Vol. 2: *When Moby Dick Blows;* Vol. 3: *After Moby Dick.* Translated by Raymond Chamberlain. Toronto: Coach House Press, 1985.

Bersianik, Louky [Lucille Durand]. *L'Euguélionne.* Montréal: Editions La Presse, 1976. *The Euguélionne.* Translated by Gerry Denis, Alison Hewitt, Donna Murray, and Martha O'Brien. Victoria: Press Porcépic, 1981.

————. *Le Pique-nique sur l'Acropole.* Montréal: VLB Editeur, 1979. (Picnic on the Acropolis)

Bessette, Gérard. *Le Libraire.* Montréal: Le Cercle du Livre de France, 1960. *Not for Every Eye.* Translated by Glen Shortliffe. Toronto: Macmillan, 1962.

————. *L'Incubation.* Montréal: Librairie Déom, 1965. *Incubation.* Translated by Glen Shortliffe. Toronto: Macmillan, 1967.

————. *Les Anthropoïdes.* Montréal: Editions La Presse, 1977. (The anthropoids)

————. *Le Semestre.* Montréal: Editions Québec/Amérique, 1979. (The semester)

Blais, Marie-Claire. *Une Saison dans la vie d'Emmanuel.* Montréal: Editions du Jour, 1965. *A Season in the Life of Emmanuel.* Translated by Derek Coltman. New York: Farrar, Straus & Giroux, 1966.

————. *Manuscrits de Pauline Archange.* Montréal: Editions du Jour, 1968. *Manuscripts of Pauline Archange.* Translated by Derek Coltman. New York: Farrar, Straus & Giroux, 1970.

————. *Vivre! Vivre!* Montréal: Editions du Jour, 1969. Vol. 2 of *Manuscrits de Pauline Archange.* (Part 2 of *Manuscripts . . .* in the translation listed above.)

————. *Les Apparences.* Montréal: Editions du Jour, 1970. Vol. 3 of *Manuscrits. . . . Dürer's Angel.* Translated by David Lobdell. Vancouver: Talonbooks, 1976. Vol. 3 of *Manuscripts. . . .*

————. *Le Loup.* Montréal: Editions du Jour, 1972. *The Wolf.* Translated by Sheila Fischman. Toronto: McClelland & Stewart, 1974.

————. *Les Nuits de l'Underground.* Montréal: Editions Internationales Alain Stanké, 1978. *Nights in the Underground: An Exploration of Love.* Translated by Ray Ellenwood. Don Mills, Ont.: Musson Book Co., 1979.

————. *Le Sourd dans la ville.* Montréal: Editions Internationales Alain Stanké, 1979. *Deaf to the City.* Translated by Carol Dunlop. Toronto: Lester & Orpen Dennys, 1981.

————. *Visions d'Anna.* Montréal: Editions Internationales Alain Stanké, 1982. *Anna's World.* Translated by Sheila Fischman. Toronto: Lester & Orpen Dennys, 1985.

Boucher de Boucherville, Pierre-Georges-Prévost. *Une de perdue, deux de trouvées.* Montréal: Eusèbe Sénécal, 1874. First appeared in *L'Album littéraire et musical de la Minerve,* 1849–1851, and in *La Revue canadienne,* 1864–1865. (One lost, two found)

Bourassa, Napoléon. *Jacques et Marie.* Montréal: Eusèbe Sénécal, 1866. First appeared in *La Revue canadienne,* 1865–1866. (Jacques and Marie)

Carrier, Roch. *La Guerre, yes sir!* Montréal: Editions du Jour, 1968. *La Guerre, Yes sir!* Translated by Sheila Fischman. Toronto: House of Anansi, 1970.

————. *Floralie, où es-tu?* Montréal: Editions du Jour, 1969. *Floralie, Where Are You?* Translated by Sheila Fischman. Toronto: House of Anansi, 1971.

————. *Il est par là, le soleil.* Montréal: Editions du Jour, 1970. *Is it the Sun, Philibert?* Translated by Sheila Fischman. Toronto: House of Anansi, 1972.

————. *Le Deux-millième Etage.* Montréal: Editions du Jour, 1973. *They Won't Demolish Me!* Translated by Sheila Fischman. Toronto: House of Anansi, 1974.

————. *La Dame qui avait des chaînes aux chevilles.* Montréal: Editions Internationales Alain Stanké, 1981. *Lady with Chains.* Translated by Sheila Fischman. Toronto: House of Anansi, 1984.

Charbonneau, Robert. *Ils posséderont la terre.* Montréal: Editions de l'Arbre, 1941. First appeared in *La Relève,* 1938, 1940, 1941. (They shall inherit the earth)

————. *Les Désirs et les jours.* Montréal: Editions de l'Arbre, 1948. (Desires and days)

Conan, Laure [Félicité Angers]. *Angéline de Montbrun.* Québec: Léger Brousseau, 1884. First appeared in *La Revue canadienne,* 1881–1882. *Angéline de Montbrun.* Translated by Yves Brunelle. Toronto: University of Toronto Press, 1974.

Ducharme, Réjean. *L'Avalée des avalés.* Paris: Gallimard, 1966. *The Swallower Swallowed.* Translated by Barbara Bray. London: Hamish Hamilton, 1968.

————. *Le Nez qui voque.* Paris: Gallimard, 1967. (Equivocation)

————. *L'Océantume.* Paris: Gallimard, 1968. (An ocean of bitterness)

————. *La Fille de Christophe Colomb.* Paris: Gallimard, 1969. (Christopher Columbus's daughter)

——. *L'Hiver de force.* Paris: Gallimard, 1973. *Wild to Mild: A Tale.* Translated by Robert Guy Scully. Saint-Lambert, Québec: Editions Héritage, 1980.

——. *"Fragment inédit de* l'Océantume." In *Etudes Françaises* 11, nos. 3–4 (octobre 1975):227–46. (Special issue titled *Avez-vous relu Ducharme?*)

——. *Les Enfantômes.* Paris: Gallimard, 1976. (The ghosts of childhood)

Durand, Lucille. See Bersianik, Louky.

Elie, Robert. *La Fin des songes.* Montréal: Librairie Beauchemin, 1950. *Farewell My Dreams.* Translated by Irene Coffin. Toronto: Ryerson Press, 1954.

Ferron, Jacques. *Cotnoir.* Montréal: Editions d'Orphée, 1962. *Dr. Cotnoir.* Translated by Pierre Cloutier. Montreal: Harvest House, 1973.

——. *La Nuit.* Montréal: Editions Parti Pris, 1965. (Night)

——. *La Charrette.* Montréal: Editions Hurtubise/HMH, 1968. *The Cart.* Translated by Ray Ellenwood. Toronto: Exile Editions, 1981.

——. *Le Ciel de Québec.* Montréal: Editions du Jour, 1969. *The Penniless Redeemer.* Translated by Ray Ellenwood. Toronto: Exile Editions, 1984.

——. *L'Amélanchier.* Montréal: Editions du Jour, 1970. *The Juneberry Tree.* Translated by Raymond Chamberlain. Montreal: Harvest House, 1975.

——. *Le Salut de l'Irlande.* Montréal: Editions du Jour, 1970. (Ireland's salvation)

——. *Le Saint-Elias.* Montréal: Editions du Jour, 1972. *The Saint-Elias.* Translated by Pierre Cloutier. Montreal: Harvest House, 1975.

——. *Les Confitures de coings et autres textes.* Montréal: Editions Parti pris, 1972. *Quince Jam.* Translated by Ray Ellenwood. Toronto: Coach House Press, 1977.

Gérin-Lajoie, Antoine. *Jean Rivard le défricheur, récit de la vie réelle.* Montréal: Jean-Baptiste Rolland, 1874. First appeared in *Le Canadien, Les Soirées canadiennes, Le Journal de l'instruction publique,* 1862. *Jean Rivard.* Translated by Vida Bruce. Toronto: McClelland & Stewart, 1977.

——. *Jean Rivard économiste.* Montréal: Jean-Baptiste Rolland, 1876. First appeared in *Le Foyer canadien* and *Le Journal de l'instruction publique,* 1864. (McClelland & Stewart translation cited above includes *Jean Rivard, Settler* and *Jean Rivard, Economist*).

Godbout, Jacques. *L'Aquarium.* Paris: Editions du Seuil, 1962. (The aquarium)

——. *Le Couteau sur la table.* Paris: Editions du Seuil, 1965. *Knife on the Table.* Translated by Penny Williams. Toronto: McClelland & Stewart, 1976.

————. *Salut Galarneau!* Paris: Editions du Seuil, 1967. *Hail Galarneau!* Translated by Alan Brown. Toronto: Longmans, 1970.

————. *D'Amour, P.Q.* Paris: Editions du Seuil, 1972. (Thomas d'Amour, P.Q.)

————. *L'Isle au dragon.* Paris: Editions du Seuil, 1976. *Dragon Island.* Translated by David Ellis. Don Mills, Ont.: Musson Book Co., 1978.

————. *Les Têtes à Papineau.* Paris: Editions du Seuil, 1981. (Papineau, the bicephalous monster)

Grignon, Claude-Henri. *Un Homme et son péché.* Montréal: Editions du Totem, 1933. *The Woman and the Miser.* Translated by Yves Brunelle. Montreal: Harvest House, 1978.

Guèvremont, Germaine. *Le Survenant.* Montréal: Librairie Beauchemin, 1945. Revised 1968 version: Montréal: Editions Fides, 1974. *The Outlander.* Translated by Eric Sutton. Toronto: McClelland & Stewart, 1978, including *Marie-Didace.*

————. *Marie-Didace.* Montréal: Librairie Beauchemin, 1947. (See above.)

Hébert, Anne. *Les Chambres de bois.* Paris: Editions du Seuil, 1958. *The Silent Rooms.* Translated by Kathy Mezei. Don Mills, Ont.: Musson Book Co., 1974.

————. *Kamouraska.* Paris: Editions du Seuil, 1970. *Kamouraska.* Translated by Norman Shapiro. Don Mills, Ont.: PaperJacks, 1974.

————. *Les Enfants du sabbat.* Paris: Editions du Seuil, 1975. *Children of the Black Sabbath.* Translated by Carol Dunlop. Don Mills, Ont.: Musson Book Co., 1977.

————. *Les Fous de Bassan.* Paris: Editions du Seuil, 1982. *In the Shadow of the Wind.* Translated by Sheila Fischman. Don Mills, Ont.: Stoddart, 1983.

Hémon, Louis. *Maria Chapdelaine.* Montréal: J.-A. Lefebvre, 1916. First appeared in *Le Temps,* 1914. *Maria Chapdelaine: A Tale of the Lake St. John Country.* Translated by W. H. Blake. Toronto: Macmillan, 1973.

Laberge, Albert. *La Scouine.* Montréal: private edition, 1918. First appeared as short stories between 1903 and 1916. *Bitter Bread.* Translated by Conrad Dion. Montreal: Harvest House, 1977.

Langevin, André. *Evadé de la nuit.* Montréal: Le Cercle du Livre de France, 1951. (Night escape)

————. *Poussière sur la ville.* Montréal: Le Cercle du Livre de France, 1953. *Dust over the City.* Translated by John Latrobe & Robert Gottlieb. Toronto: McClelland & Stewart, 1974.

————. *Le Temps des hommes.* Montréal: Le Cercle du Livre de France, 1956. (Man's reckoning)

La Rocque, Gilbert. *Serge d'entre les morts.* Montréal: VLB Editeur, 1976. (Serge from among the dead)

————. *Les Masques.* Montréal: Editions Québec/Amérique, 1980. (The masks)

Lemelin, Roger. *Au pied de la pente douce.* Montréal: Editions de l'Arbre, 1944. *The Town Below.* Translated by Samuel Putnam. Toronto: McClelland & Stewart, 1961.

————. *Les Plouffe.* Québec: Editions Bélisle, 1948. *The Plouffe Family.* Translated by Mary Finch. Toronto: McClelland & Stewart, 1975.

Maheux-Forcier, Louise. *Amadou.* Montréal: Le Cercle du Livre de France, 1963. (Fire)

————. *L'Ile joyeuse.* Montréal: Le Cercle du Livre de France, 1964. (The joyous island)

————. *Une Forêt pour Zoé.* Montréal: Le Cercle du Livre de France, 1969. (A forest for Zoé)

Panneton, Philippe. See Ringuet.

Paradis, Suzanne. *Les Cormorans.* Québec: Editions Garneau, 1968. (The cormorants)

————. *Emmanuelle en noir.* Québec: Editions Garneau, 1971. (Emmanuelle in black)

————. *Quand la terre était toujours jeune.* Québec: Editions Garneau, 1974. "When the Earth Was Still Young." Translated by Basil Kingstone. *Canadian Fiction Magazine* 26 (1977):61–145.

————. *L'Eté sera chaud.* Québec: Editions Garneau, 1975. (A hot summer in store)

————. *Un Portrait de Jeanne Joron.* Québec: Editions Garneau, 1977. (A portrait of Jeanne Joron)

————. *Miss Charlie.* Montréal: Editions Leméac, 1979. (Miss Charlie)

Ringuet [Philippe Panneton]. *Trente Arpents.* Paris: Editions Flammarion, 1938. *Thirty Acres.* Translated by Dorothea & Felix Walter. Toronto: McClelland & Stewart, 1970.

Roy, Gabrielle. *Bonheur d'occasion.* Montréal: Société des Editions Pascal, 1945. *The Tin Flute.* Translated by Alan Brown. Toronto: McClelland & Stewart, 1980; trans. based on 1977 revised edition.

————. *La Petite Poule d'eau.* Montréal: Librairie Beauchemin, 1950. *Where Nests the Water Hen.* Translated by Harry Binsse. Toronto: McClelland & Stewart, 1961.

————. *Alexandre Chenevert.* Montréal: Librairie Beauchemin, 1954. *The Cashier.* Translated by Harry Binsse. Toronto: McClelland & Stewart, 1963.

————. *La Montagne secrète.* Montréal: Librairie Beauchemin, 1961. *The Hidden Mountain.* Translated by Harry Binsse. Toronto: McClelland & Stewart, 1974.

————. *La Route d'Altamont.* Montréal: Editions Hurtubise/HMH, 1966. *The Road Past Altamont.* Translated by Joyce Marshall. Toronto: McClelland & Stewart, 1966.

Savard, Félix-Antoine. *Menaud, maître draveur.* Québec: Editions Garneau, 1937. *Master of the River.* Translated by Richard Howard. Montreal: Harvest House, 1976; trans. based on 1965 revised edition.

————. *L'Abatis.* Montréal: Editions Fides, 1943. (The felling)

————. *La Minuit.* Montréal: Editions Fides, 1948. (Christmas eve)

Thériault, Yves. *Aaron.* Québec: Institut littéraire du Québec, 1954. (Aaron)

————. *Agaguk.* Québec: Institut littéraire du Québec, 1958. *Agaguk.* Translated by Miriam Chapin. Toronto: Ryerson Press, 1963.

————. *Cul-de-sac.* Québec: Institut littéraire du Québec, 1961. *Kesten* and *Cul-de-Sac.* Translated by Gwendolyn Moore. Toronto: Clarke, Irwin & Co., 1973.

SECONDARY SOURCES

Baillargeon, Samuel. *Littérature canadienne-française.* Montréal: Editions Fides, 1957. Anthology of selected extracts with commentary.

Belleau, André. *Le Romancier fictif: essai sur la représentation de l'écrivain dans le roman québécois.* Sillery: Presses de l'Université du Québec, 1980. Notable study of the author-as-character in novels of Roy, Lemelin, Bessette, Godbout; less extensive treatment of Aquin, V.-L. Beaulieu, Ducharme.

Bessette, Gérard. *Une littérature en ébullition.* Montréal: Editions du Jour, 1968. Lengthy essays on Grignon, Roy, Thériault.

Bessette, Gérard, Lucien Geslin, and Charles Parent. *Histoire de la littérature canadienne-française.* Ville d'Anjou: Centre Educatif et Culturel, 1968. Anthology of selected extracts with commentary.

Boucher, Jean-Pierre. *Instantanés de la condition québécoise.* Montréal: Editions Hurtubise/HMH, 1977.

Boynard-Frot, Janine. *Un matriarcat en procès: analyse systématique de romans canadiens-français, 1860–1960.* Montréal: Presses de l'Université de Montréal, 1982. Sociohistorical study of cultural representation in the Quebec agrarian novel, specifically woman's "space" in it.

Brochu, André. *L'Instance critique.* Montréal: Editions Leméac, 1974.

Charbonneau, Robert. *Connaissance du personnage.* Montréal: Editions de l'Arbre, 1944. Important document in history of Quebec literary criticism.

Collet, Paulette. *L'Hiver dans le roman canadien-français.* Québec: Presses de l'Université Laval, 1965. Social aspects of winter life in nineteenth- and twentieth-century novels; casually discursive discussion.

Ducrocq-Poirier, Madeleine. *Le Roman canadien de langue française de 1860 à 1958.* Paris: Nizet, 1978. Lengthy treatise of specific novels and works; excellent bio-bibliographies for all authors studied.

Dumont, Fernand, and Charles Falardeau, eds. *Littérature et société canadiennes-françaises.* Québec: Presses de l'Université Laval, 1964. Literature as social expression; themes of love, religion, revolt treated in separate essays.

Esprit Créateur 23 (1983). Special issue devoted to Quebec novel.

Falardeau, Jean-Charles. *Notre société et son roman.* Montréal: Editions Hurtubise/HMH, 1972. Ideologies and social themes in the novel; specific essays on Chauveau, Gérin-Lajoie, Charbonneau, Lemelin.

French Review 53, no. 6 (May 1980). Special issue devoted to Quebec literature.

Gauvin, Lise. *"Parti pris" littéraire.* Montréal: Presses de Université de Montréal, 1975. Important tract on this social and literary movement of the 1960s.

Grandpré, Pierre de, et al. *Histoire de la littérature française du Québec,* 4 vols. Montréal: Librairie Beauchemin, 1967–1969. Anthology of selected extracts with commentary.

Imbert, Patrick. *Roman québécois contemporain et clichés. Ottawa: Presse de l'Université d'Ottawa,* 1983.

Lectures européennes de la littérature québécoise. (Actes du Colloque international de Montréal, avril 1981.) Montréal: Editions Leméac, 1982. Section on the novel contains studies of Victor-Lévy Beaulieu, Jacques Godbout, Ringuet.

Lemire, Maurice. *Les Grands Thèmes nationalistes du roman canadien-français.* Québec: Presses de l'Université Laval, 1970.

Littérature canadienne-française. (Conférence J.-A. de Sève, 1–10.) Montréal: Presses de l'Université de Montréal, 1969.

Mailhot, Laurent. *La Littérature québécoise.* Paris: Presses Universitaires de France, 1974. ("Que sais-je?") Concise overview of French-Canadian literature.

Major, André. *Parti pris: idéologies et littérature.* Montréal: Editions Hurtubise/HMH, 1979. Intensive inquiry into the politics and aesthetics of the "Parti pris" group in the arts.

Marcotte, Gilles. *Le Roman à l'imparfait: essais sur le roman québécois d'aujourd'hui.* Montréal: Editions La Presse, 1976. Rambling essays on Bessette, Blais, Godbout, Ducharme.

————, ed. *Présence de la critique: critique et littérature contemporaines au Canada français.* Montréal: Editions Hurtubise/HMH, 1966. Collection of reviews of works of some fifteen novelists; interesting only for view of critics' reactions to novels at time of their appearance.

Ménard, Jean. *La Vie littéraire au Canada français.* Ottawa: Editions de l'Université d'Ottawa, 1971.

Modern Language Studies 6, no. 2 (Fall 1976). Special issue devoted to Quebec literature.

Paradis, Suzanne. *Femme fictive, femme réelle: le personnage féminin dans le roman féminin canadien-français, 1884–1966.* Québec: Editions Garneau, 1966. Penetrating essays; essential for diachronic and synchronic study of topic.

Petit manuel de littérature québécoise. Etudes Françaises 13, nos. 3–4 (octobre 1977). Special issue devoted to Quebec literature.

Poulin, Gabrielle. *Romans du pays 1968–1979.* Montréal: Editions Bellarmin, 1980. Study of some thirty novelists; many are given armchair critic approach; longer chapters devoted to André Major, Carrier, V.-L. Beaulieu lack serious critical focus.

Robidoux, Réjean, and André Renaud. *Le Roman canadien-français du vingtième siècle.* Ottawa: Editions de l'Université d'Ottawa, 1966. Studies of fourteen nineteenth- and twentieth-century novelists according to thematic preoccupations of each.

Romanciers du Québec. Québec: Editions Québec Français, 1980. Interviews with ten leading twentieth-century novelists culled from the journal *Québec Français* between 1974 and 1980; included is a brief biography and critical article for each.

Servais-Maquoi, Mireille. *Le Roman de la terre au Québec.* Québec: Presses de l'Université Laval, 1974. Study of this important theme from Lacombe to Guèvremont.

Tougas, Gérard. *Destin littéraire du Québec.* Montréal: Editions Québec/Amérique, 1982.

————. *La Littérature canadienne-française.* Paris: Presses Universitaires de France, 1960. Overview of French-Canadian literature; book is marred by judgmental, biased attitudes and comments; not recommended to beginning students of the literature.

Warwick, Jack. *The Long Journey.* Toronto: University of Toronto Press, 1968. Treats theme of "call of the North" in nineteenth- and twentieth-century prose; specific chapters on allied themes of quest, regeneration, revolt.

Yale French Studies 65 (1983). Special issue devoted to Quebec literature.

Index

Alienation, 19, 28–29, 32–33, 44–46, 48–
49, *51–55*, 56–58, *61–67*, 69–71, 74–
84, 88–89, 100, *110–13*, 134–35, 139,
140

Angers, Félicité. *See* Conan, Laure

Anticlericalism, 30, 48–49, 54–55, 63–64,
107–9, 122

Aquin, Hubert, *Antiphonaire, L' (The Antiphonary); Prochain épisode (Prochain épisode);
Trou de mémoire (Blackout)*, 98–106, 124,
143

Aubert de Gaspé, Philippe (father), *Anciens
Canadiens, Les (Canadians of Old)*, 8, *12*,
16

Aubert de Gaspé, Philippe (son), *Chercheur de
trésor ou l'influence d'un livre, Le* (The treasure seeker or the influence of a book), 8

Authenticity, search for, 1, *45–49*, *52–53*,
56–58, 60–61, 63–64, 69, 74–84, 90–
97, 127–28, 130, 136, 138, 140, 143

Baillargeon, Pierre, *Commerce* (Commerce);
Médisances de Claude Perrin, Les (The cynicism of Claude Perrin), 41, *45–46*, 47

Beauchemin, Yves, *Matou, Le (The Tomcat),
136–41*, 143

Beaugrand, Honoré, *Jeanne la fileuse* (Jeanne
the spinner), 8, *12*, 17

Beaulieu, Victor-Lévy, *Don Quichotte de la démanche (Don Quixote in Nighttown); Grands-
pères, Les (The Grandfathers); Jos Connaissant
(Jos Connaissant); Monsieur Melville (Monsieur Melville); Nuitte de Malcolm Hudd, La
(The night of Malcolm Hudd); Rêve québécois, Un (A Québécois Dream)*, 73, *122–26*,
143

Bersianik, Louky, *Euguélionne, L' (The Eugue-
lionne); Pique-nique sur l'Acropole, Le* (Picnic
on the Acropolis), *130–33*, 143

Bessette, Gérard, *Anthropoïdes, Les* (The anthropoids); *Incubation, L' (Incubation); Libraire, Le (Not for Every Eye); Semestre, Le*
(The semester), 67–74, 143

Blais, Marie-Claire, *Apparences, Les (Dürer's
Angel); Loup, Le (The Wolf); Manuscrits de
Pauline Archange (Manuscripts of Pauline Ar-

change); Nuits de l'Underground, Les (Nights
in the Underground: An Exploration of Love);
Saison dans la vie d'Emmanuel, Une (A Season in the Life of Emmanuel); Sourd dans la
ville, Le (Deaf to the City); Visions d'Anna
(Anna's World); Vivre! Vivre!* (part two of
Manuscrits), *106–12*

Borduas, Paul Emile, *Refus global*, 142

Boucher de Boucherville, Pierre-Georges-Prévost, *Une de perdue, deux de trouvées* (One
lost, two found), 8, *9–10*

Bourassa, Napoléon, *Jacques et Marie* (Jacques
and Marie), 8, *9–10*, 16

Breton, André, 142

Brossard, Nicole, 73

Buies, Arthur, 17

Call of the wilderness, 11, 20, 23, *38–40*,
122

Carrier, Roch, *Dame qui avait des chaines aux
chevilles, La (Lady with Chains); Deux-mil-
liéme Etage, Le (They Won't Demolish Me!);
Floralie, où es-tu? (Floralie, Where are
You?); Guerre, yes sir!, La (La Guerre, Yes
Sir!); Il est par là, le soleil (Is it the Sun,
Philibert?)*, *118–22*, 143

Cartier, Jacques, 1, 6

Casgrain, Henri-Raymond, Abbé, 11, 16,
19

Champlain, Samuel de, 1, 6

Charbonneau, Robert, *Désirs et les jours, Les*
(Desires and days); *Ils posséderont la terre*
(They shall inherit the earth), 3, 41, *42–
45*, 47

Chateaubriand, François René de, 16

Chauveau, Pierre-Joseph-Olivier, *Charles
Guérin* (Charles Guérin), 2, 8, 16

Childhood and adolescence, 3, 30, *43–48*,
54, 60–61, 66, 70, *90–97*, 106, 108–9,
111, *112–16*, 133–35, 137, 143

Church influence, 1–3, 5–6, 8, 10–11, 14,
16–23, 26–27, 51, 63–64, 67–69, 88,
90–91, 93, 96–97, 142

Cité Libre (Free City), 142

Conan, Laure, *Angéline de Montbrun (Angéline
de Montbrun)*, 8–9, *12*, *13–16*, 17, 20

Confederation Act of 1867, 1
Crémazie, Octave, 16, 17

Desrosiers, Léo-Paul, *Nord-Sud* (North-South); *Engagés du grand portage, Les (The Making of Nicolas Montour)*, 19, 24, 32
Doutre, Joseph, *Fiancés de 1812, Les* (The fiancés of 1812), 8, 17
Ducharme, Réjean, *Avalée des avalés, L' (The Swallower Swallowed); Bons Débarras, Les* (Good riddance); *Enfantômes, Les* (The ghosts of Childhood); *Fille de Christophe Colomb, La* (Christopher Columbus's daughter); *Hiver de force, L' (Wild to Mild: A Tale); Nez qui voque, Le* (Equivocation); *Océantume, L' (An ocean of bitterness)*, 112–18, 143
Durand, Lucille. *See* Bersianik, Louky

Elie, Robert, *Fin des songes, La (Farewell My Dreams)*, 41, 46–48
Ecole littéraire de Montréal, L', 17
Ecole Patriotique de Québec, L', 16–17

Female-male roles, 16, 54, 57–58, 60, 65, 66–67, 78–80, 91, 106–11, 127–28, 130–33, 143
Ferron, Jaques, *Amélanchier, L' (The Juneberry Tree); Charrette, La (The Cart); Ciel de Québec, Le (The Penniless Redeemer); Confitures de coings, Les (Quince Jam); Cotnoir (Dr. Cotnoir); Nuit, La (Night); Saint-Elias, Le (The Saint-Elias); Salut de l'Irlande, Le* (Ireland's salvation), 73, 84–90, 143
Foyer canadien, Le, 16
Fréchette, Louis, 17
Freud, Sigmund, 73, 131
Front de Libération du Québec, 80, 85

Garneau, François-Xavier, *Histoire du Canada* (History of Canada), 8, 13, 16, 18, 23
Geography, *1–3, 9, 11–12,* 17, 19, *20–21,* 31, *37–40, 49–50,* 56, 59, 65, *76–78, 80–81,* 85, 89
Gérin-Lajoie, Antoine, *Jean Rivard économiste (Jean Rivard, Economist); Jean Rivard le défricheur (Jean Rivard, Settler)*, 2, 8, *12–13,* 17, 31
Girard, Rodolphe, *Marie Calumet* (Marie Calumet), 19
Giroux, André, *Au-delà des visages* (Beyond faces), 41
Godbout, Jacques, *Aquarium, L'* (The aquarium); *Couteau sur la table, Le (Knife on the Table); D'Amour, P.Q.* (Thomas D'Amour, P.Q.); *Isle au dragon, L' (Dragon Island); Salut Galarneau! (Hail Galarneau!); Têtes à Papineau, Les* (Papineau, the bicephalous monster), 74–84, 88, 143
Grignon, Claude-Henri, *Homme et son péché, Un (The Woman and the Miser)*, 17, 19, 22, *24–26,* 27, 28
Groulx, Lionel, Abbé, *Appel de la race, L'* (The call of the race), 18, 19, 23, 51
Guèvremont, Germaine, *Marie-Didace (Marie-Didace); Survenant, Le (The Outlander)*, 24, 28, *31–34*
Hébert, Anne, *Chambres de bois, Les (The Silent Rooms); Enfants du sabbat, Les (Children of the Black Sabbath); Fous de Bassan, Les (In the Shadow of the Wind); Héloïse* (Heloise); *Kamouraska (Kamouraska)*, 59–67, 73, 85, 127, 128, 143
Hémon, Louis, *Maria Chapdelaine (Maria Chapdelaine: A Tale of the Lake St. John Country)*, 2, 19, *20–21,* 31
Hertel, François, *Anatole Laplante, curieux homme* (Anatole Laplante, strange man), 41
Hugo, Victor, 16, 124

Institut Canadien, L', 17
Ionesco, Eugène, 117
Irony, 68, *72–74,* 78, *81–82,* 100, *104–5,* 108, 118, 137, 139

Jarry, Alfred, 117

Kerouac, Jack, 124

Laberge, Albert, *Scouine, La (Bitter Bread)*, 17, 19, *21–23,* 24, 25, 27, 28
Lacan, Jacques, 131
Lacombe, Patrice, *Terre paternelle, La* (The fatherland), 2, 8,
Langevin, André, *Evadé de la nuit* (Night escape); *Poussière sur la ville (Dust over the City); Temps des hommes, Le* (Man's reckoning), *51–55*
La Rocque, Gilbert, *Masques, Les* (The masks); *Serge d'entre les morts* (Serge from among the dead), 73, *133–36*
Lautréamont, 177
Laval University, 6
Leclerc, Gilles, *Journal d'un inquisiteur* (Diary of an inquisitor), 51
Le Clézio, J. M. G., 117
Lemay, Pamphile, *Picounoc le maudit* (Picounoc the damned), 8

Lemelin, Roger, *Au pied de la pente douce (The Town Below); Plouffe, Les (The Plouffe Family)*, 2, 19, 29–31, 48
Lévesque, René, 3
Liberté, 73, 77
Loranger, Jean-Aubert, 17

Maheux-Forcier, Louise, *Amadou* (Fire); *Forêt pour Zoé, Une* (A forest for Zoé); *Ile joyeuse, L'* (The joyous island), 90–97, 143
Marie de l'Incarnation, Soeur, 1, 6
Marmette, Joseph, *François de Bienville* (François de Bienville), 8
Melville, Herman, 124
Miron, Gaston, *Vie agonique, La (The Agonized Life)*, 51
Montcalm, de Saint-Véran (Louis, marquis de), 1
Montesquieu, Charles de Secondat, baron de la Brède, 133

Nationalism (Quebec as a "nation"), 2–4, 8, 10, 16–17, 19, 23–24, 26, 30, 45, 50–51, 57, 74–84, 87, 88, 126; *see also* Possession-dispossession, and Religious patriotism
Nelligan, Emile, 17
"New Novelists," 3, 50, 70, 71, 98, 104, 124
Nodier, Charles, 16
Novels of the land, 2, 10–13, 19, 20–24, 26–28, 31–34, 49; *see also* Rural-urban polarity

Panneton, Philippe. *See* Ringuet
Paradis, Suzanne, *Cormorans, Les* (The Cormorants); *Emmanuelle en noir* (Emmanuelle in black); *Eté sera chaud, L'* (A hot summer in store); *Femme fictive, femme réelle: le personnage féminin dans le roman canadien-français, 1884–1966* (Fictional woman, real woman: female characters in French-Canadian novels, 1884–1966); *Miss Charlie* (Miss Charlie); *Portrait de Jeanne Joron, Un* (A Portrait of Jeanne Joron); *Quand la terre était toujours jeune* ("When the Earth Was Still Young"), 126–30, 141n1, 143
Parti pris ("set purpose"), 50, 142
Parti québécois, 3, 80
Plato, *Symposium*, 131
Poeticized prose, 21, 26–27, 31–34, 48, 59–67, 92–94, 104–5, 109, 111–12, 117, 122, 126–30, 143

Possession-dispossession, 3, 10, 13, 24, 29, 51, 53–54, 57, 60, 63, 65, 75–82, 84, 87–90, 100, 115, 119, 125–26, 136, 139–40, 143; *see also* Nationalism, and Religious patriotism
Potvin, Damase, 19, 21–22
Proust, Marcel, *A la recherche du temps perdu (Remembrance of Things Past)*, 38

Quebec Act of 1791, 6
Quebec-United States relations, 6, 13, 20, 23–24, 29, 65, 77–79, 81–82, 84, 90, 115, 125, 137, 139
Queneau, Raymond, 117
"Quiet Revolution," 2–3, 24, 50–51, 60, 67, 75, 77, 80

Rabelais, François, 117, 132
Reality vs fantasy, 8, 12, 29–30, 35, 37–38, 46–48, 50, 56–57, 61–62, 64–66, 72–74, 82–85, 88, 90–101, 105, 114, 117, 119, 122–24, 125, 127–39, 143
Relations des Jésuites, 1
Religious patriotism, 2, 6, 10–14, 16–19, 20–23, 26–27, 142; *see also* Nationalism, and Possession-dispossession
Ringuet, *Trente Arpents (Thirty Acres)*, 19, 22, 24, 27–29, 33
Robbe-Grillet, Alain, 50, 70, 124
Roquebrune, Robert de, 19, 24
Routhier, Adolphe-Basile, 11, 17
Roy, Camille, Abbé, 19, 86
Roy, Gabrielle, *Alexandre Chenevert (The Cashier); Bonheur d'occasion (The Tin Flute); Montagne secrète, La (The Hidden Mountain); Petite Poule d'eau, La (Where Nests the Water Hen); Route d'Altamont, La (The Road Past Altamont)*, 2, 19, 34–41, 48
Royal Proclamation of 1763, 6
Rural-urban polarity, 2, 13, 19, 22, 27–29, 89–90, 107, 120, 126; *see also* Novels of the land, and Urban novel

Saint-Denys Garneau, 85
Sarraute, Nathalie, 50
Satire, 29–31, 59, 73–74, 78, 82, 85, 118, 130–32, 135, 140
Savard, Félix-Antoine, *Menaud, maître draveur (Master of the River)*, 24, 26–27
Simon, Claude, 70
Société du parler français, La, 19
Socrates, 131
Soirées canadiennes, Les, 16

Soirées de l'Ecole littéraire de Montréal, Les, 17
Soirées du château de Ramezay, Les, 17

Tardivel, Jules-Paul, 11, 17
Text as game, *71–72,* 83, *98–106, 113–118,* 123, 142, 143
Thériault, Yves, *Aaron* (Aaron); *Agaguk* *(Agaguk); Cul-de-sac (Cul-de-sac),* 55–59
Treaty of Paris, 1

Trudeau, Pierre Elliott, 73, 139–40

Urban novel, 2, 19, *29–31, 35–38,* 49, 56–57, 108–9, 110–11, 121; *see also* Rural-urban polarity

Writing, act of, *45–46,* 50, 74, *78–84,* 89, *98–106, 107–10, 114–18, 122–24, 128–29,* 135

Vian, Boris, 117